Co Antrim

Edited by Angela Fairbrace

First published in Great Britain in 2008 by:
Young Writers
Remus House
Coltsfoot Drive
Peterborough
PE2 9JX
Telephone: 01733 890066
Website: www.youngwriters.co.uk

SB ISBN 978-1 84431 645 8

Foreword

Young Writers was established in 1991 and has been passionately devoted to the promotion of reading and writing in children and young adults ever since. The quest continues today. Young Writers remains as committed to the nurturing of poetic and literary talent as ever.

This year's Young Writers competition has proven as vibrant and dynamic as ever and we are delighted to present a showcase of the best poetry from across the UK and in some cases overseas. Each poem has been selected from a wealth of *Little Laureates 2008* entries before ultimately being published in this, our seventeenth primary school poetry series.

Once again, we have been supremely impressed by the overall quality of the entries we have received. The imagination, energy and creativity which has gone into each young writer's entry made choosing the poems a challenging and often difficult but ultimately hugely rewarding task - the general high standard of the work submitted ensured this opportunity to bring their poetry to a larger appreciative audience.

We sincerely hope you are pleased with this final collection and that you will enjoy *Little Laureates 2008 Co Antrim* for many years to come.

Contents

Thomas Ferguson (9)	19
Joel Adams (9)	19
Philip Gregg (9)	20
Susannah Graham (8)	20
David Stevenson (8)	20
Claire Adams (9)	21
Stuart Miller (11)	21
Shane Gibson (9)	21
Emma Purdy (9)	22
Chloe Kernohan (10)	22
Sarah Eccles (9)	23
Kathleen Witherspoon (9)	23
Aaron Smyrell (10)	24
Alyson Erwin (8)	24
Lois Cupples (11)	25
Jonathan Loughridge (9)	25
Jade Lamont (9)	26
Kara Taylor (9)	26
Jordan McClean (10)	27
Rebecca Marcus (8)	27
Amy McAllister (10)	28
Shannon Erwin (8)	28
Emma Heron (10)	29
Emily Erwin (7)	29
Megan Montgomery (10)	30
Nicole Turtle (9)	30
Thomas Bell (11)	31
Alex Marshall (10)	31
Jonathan Cummings (10)	32
Steven Galloway (11)	32
Caitlin Lennon (9)	33
Grace McNeill (8)	33
Jessica Newell (8)	34
Andrew McKee (8)	34
Courtney Lewis (8)	34
Susie Neeson (7)	35
Caitlin Caldwell (9)	35
Morgen Blair (7)	35
Naomi Crawford (8)	36
Laura Craig (7)	36

Buick Memorial Primary School, Cullybackey

Paige Murray (10)	37
Katie Farquhar (8)	37
Beth Orr (9)	38
Shannon Burnside (8)	38
Ross Evans (8)	39
Josh Weir (8)	39
Adam Taggart (8)	40
James Kennedy (7)	40
Philip Fenton (10)	41
Thomas McMurray (7)	41
Sam Hutchinson (8)	42
Ellen Harkness (8)	42
Emily Keys (10)	42
Hannah Cooke (8)	43
Georga Gordon (8)	43
Lois McCurdy (9)	43
Katie Adams (9)	44
Hannah Wylie (9)	44
Simone Lyle (9)	45
Adam McCallion (9)	45
Curtis Wylie (7)	46
Courtney McFetridge (9)	46
Jack Dixon (8)	47
Melissa Graham (9)	47
Susannah Kyle (10)	48
Samuel Craig (9)	48
Gemma Reid (9)	48
Rachel McKay (8)	49
Ben Alexander Eaton (9)	49
Sophie Ervine (9)	49
Jack Meneely (8)	50
Ashley Johnston (8)	50
Chelsea Boyd (8)	50
Robert Adair (8)	51
Joshua Galloway (7)	51
Zak Humphrey (7)	51
Rebecca Arbuthnot (9)	52
Bethany Brown (10)	52
Cathy Reid (10)	52
Catherine McMillan (10)	53

Robbie Kelly (9)	53
Emma McDowell (10)	53
Sarah Greer (10)	54
Lauren Neilly (9)	54
Lydia Simpson (9)	54
Jacob Knipe (7)	55
Amy Matthews (8)	55
Dion Houston (10)	55
Alan Arbuthnot (8)	56
Rebecca Allen (8)	56
Stuart MacGregor (8)	56
Grace McCready (8)	57
Dylan Knipe (7)	57
Harry Gaston (8)	57
Charlie Neal (8)	58
Martin Dempsey (8)	58
Isaac Simpson (7)	58
David Leetch (8)	59
Zach Wilson (7)	59
Harry Kenneway (7)	59
Corrie Reid (7)	60
Grace Henry (9)	60
Adam Mairs (10)	60
Daniel Buick (7)	61
James Simpson (9)	61
Leah Harkin (10)	61
Alistair Givens (11)	62
Amy Swann (10)	62
Moses Kirk (8)	63
Ben Gaston (11)	63
Jordan Campbell (11)	64
Adam McAuley (10)	64
Nicola Anderson (11)	65
Stuart Wylie (11)	65
Samuel Beattie (11)	66
Sam Sloan (11)	66
Daniel Stephen Brown (11)	67
Leoni Jean McQuilkin (11)	67
Robbie Campbell (11)	68
Luke Simpson (11)	68
Timothy Spence (11)	69
Suzanne Reid (8)	69

Rhianna Campbell (10)	70
Rebecca Speers (10)	70
Alan Casey (11)	71
Gareth Evans (10)	71

Bushvalley Primary School, Stranocum
Rebecca Whyte (11)	72
Ashleigh Falconer (11)	72
Abbie Patton (11)	73
Diane Ramsay (11)	73
Amy Gibson (10)	74
Clare McGurk (11)	74
Mary Patton (11)	75
Rebecca Wilkinson (10)	75

Carnalridge Primary School, Portrush
Lauren Bacon (9)	76
Angus Kelly (9)	76
Chloe Edgar (9)	77
Lauren Osbourne (9)	77
Conor McLean (9)	78
Robert Simpson (9)	79
Matthew McLaughlin (9)	80
Andrew Holmes (9)	81
Shannon Peters (9)	82
Anna Dallas (8)	83
Amber Macfarlane (8)	84
Glen Campbell (9)	85
Victoria Logan (9)	86
Caitlin Buick (8)	87
Eva McBride (8)	88
Chelsea Greer (9)	89
Shannon-Lee Mitchell (9)	90
Sarah Medcalf (8)	91
Kirsty Rebecca Millar (8)	92
Robert Downs (9)	93
Peter Minihan (8)	94
Matthew Leighton (9)	94

Carrowreagh Primary School, Ballymoney

Zara Loughridge (11)	95
Ryan Moon (10)	95
David McAneaney (11)	95
Shannon Steele (10)	96

Currie Primary School, Belfast

Demi Clarke (10)	96

Doagh Primary School, Doagh

Leah Ruddock (9)	97
Stacey Mackay (8)	97
Jack Francey (9)	98
Molly Piper (8)	98
Matthew Hamilton (9)	99
Peter Gordon (8)	99
Simon Bell (9)	100
Christopher Graham (10)	100
Amy Sands (8)	101
Hannah Magee (10)	101
Ben White (9)	102
Megan Robinson (9)	102
Stafford Lynn (10)	103

Greenisland Primary School, Greenisland

Georgia Stocker (10)	103
Peter Bothwell (11)	104
Aaron Gorman (11)	104
Scott Beattie (10)	104
Wesley Strange (11)	105
Stephen Quinn (11)	105
Jordan Pollock (11)	105
Carter McIlwain (11)	106
Lee McAlister (10)	106
Jeremy Martin (11)	106
Lesley Greer (11)	107
James Rice (11)	107
Emily Harris (11)	107
Aimee Douglas (10)	108

Greystone Primary School, Antrim

McKinney Primary School, Dundrod

Parkgate Primary School, Parkgate

St Patrick's Primary School, Rasharkin

The Poems

My Dog

My wee dog Mick,
His legs are short,
He can run very quick.
When cars come into the yard,
He makes an awful noise,
He barks and barks
And runs round in a very excited dance.
He enjoys joining in the fun with my pals,
Especially with a ball,
He can do lots of tricks
And runs away to hide the ball.
I love my little dog,
He doesn't seem to like the cat next door
And when she comes here he chases her,
And she runs for her life up a tree.

Patrick O'Boyle (9)
Braid Primary School, Broughshane

My Dreamland

My dreamland is a place where I go,
Where little streams seem to flow.
My family and friends are welcome here,
There really is no need to fear.
It's a place where you can laugh and play,
It really is a wonderful day.
The flowers have bloomed, what a beautiful sight,
The birds are a-singing, cheerful and bright.
The mountains are so tall, touching the sky,
And the trees have grown so high.
The sun is setting and so now,
I must say goodbye.

Hannah Maria O'Boyle (11)
Braid Primary School, Broughshane

Hair

When I grow up I want to be
A hairdresser - that will be me.
I will have a salon in my garden shed
And I will have it painted purple, white and red.
I will have purple chairs where my customers will sit,
I'll perm and cut and curl and dry,
I'll straighten and style, I'll bob and dye,
Every colour: blonde, brown, ginger or grey,
I'll dye the colours every day -
I'll be the best hairdresser in every way!

Emma O'Loan (10)
Braid Primary School, Broughshane

Irish Dancing

My favourite hobby is to Irish dance,
I'm skipping and hopping at every chance.
Up on my toes and turning around,
I listen carefully to the sound.

If I practise every day,
I'll get better in every way.
The steps in my head all day long,
It's like singing my favourite song.

When the festival time comes up,
I try very hard to win a cup.
All dressed up in my dancing dress,
Today I missed my spelling test.

Up onto the stage I go,
When I hear the music, I'm in full flow,
Dancing gracefully here and there,
Up and up through the air.

Irish dancing is my heart and soul
And being champion is my only goal,
So when I have to hang up my shoes,
I will certainly be full of the blues.

Katie Mulvenna (10)
Braid Primary School, Broughshane

My Dog, Dancer

Dancer is my little dog, he likes to run and play,
And me and Mammy take him for a walk every single day.
Now my little dog sleeps on the kitchen sofa
And cuddles up with his favourite toy.
He can't eat a bone but he can eat his dinner,
And he loves to run all afternoon with me,
'Til it's time to sleep.

Sinead O'Loan (9)
Braid Primary School, Broughshane

Dreams

When I lie in bed at night
I like to float away
On a cloud of dreams,
Where I can become anything I say.

I dream that I can fly,
Or play the piano in front of the Queen,
I can speak in eight different languages,
And Irish dance the best you've seen.

I dream that I live in a castle
With countless diamonds and rings.
I am such a beautiful princess,
Who will someday marry a king.

I can climb the Eiffel Tower,
Train a cheetah to sing to me,
Be a top fashion designer,
Or walk to Atlantis across the sea.

When I lie in my bed at night
I like to float away
On a cloud of dreams,
Where I can become anything I say,
Anything I say!

Michaela Best (10)
Braid Primary School, Broughshane

Gee-Gee

My little pony is my pride and joy,
She prances by with her head held high
And her eyes so bright like little stars
Twinkling in the night,
With her long soft mane
Flowing gently in
The cold autumn breeze,
Like leaves falling from the trees.

Her tail held high in the air
As she trots on by,
Her legs so strong, her hooves so hard,
She neighs so softly in the field
As the sun shines down from the silky sky.
Her nose is soft and her nostrils so wide,
As she comes closer to me I whisper,
'My little pony, my pride and joy.'

Katie McKeegan (10)
Braid Primary School, Broughshane

Popcorn

Popcorn is yellow like the sun in the sky,
Without popcorn I think I would die.
You can hear it popping when it's being made,
I wish it was served to me by a maid.

The delight of the cinema is munching popcorn,
You can hear me crunching my popcorn.
My favourite flavour of all is toffee,
But I definitely don't like coffee at *all!*

Popcorn is the best
When I take a rest,
Unlike the rest,
It is the *best!*

Pop! Pop! Pop!

Ben O'Boyle (10)
Braid Primary School, Broughshane

Football

When I got my first football
I was only two and not so tall.

Off to the field I did go,
My football skills I had to show.

A little tap and then a stroll
And with my right boot, my first goal.

No fancy kit, just a little vest,
Man of the match was Owen James Best.

Owen Best (8)
Braid Primary School, Broughshane

Fear

Fear looks like a black widow spider.
Fear tastes like fire.
Fear sounds like a cry for help.
Fear is black and red.
Fear smells like the first day of school.
Fear feels like a gun to the head.
Fear reminds me of the dark.

Peter Anthony Meehan (10)
Braidside Integrated Primary School, Ballymena

Happiness

Happiness sounds like laughing.
Happiness tastes like sweets.
Happiness reminds me of fun.
Happiness feels good to get out.
Happiness is the colour of yellow.
Happiness smells like candy.
Happiness looks like a smile on someone's face.

Becky Backus (10)
Braidside Integrated Primary School, Ballymena

Ten Menacing Munchkins!

(Inspired by 'Ten Little Schoolboys' by A A Milne)

Ten menacing Munchkins made up a rhyme,
One went crazy,
And then there were nine.

Nine menacing Munchkins saw their fate,
One ran away with fright
And then there were eight.

Eight menacing Munchkins tried to get to Heaven,
But God only let one in,
And then there were seven.

Seven menacing Munchkins tried some new tricks,
One badly hurt himself
And then there were six.

Six menacing Munchkins damaging a beehive,
One got stung
And then there were five.

Five menacing Munchkins breaking through a door,
One got five splinters
And then there were four.

Four menacing Munchkins climbing up a tree,
One tumbled down
And then there were three.

Three menacing Munchkins tying a shoe,
One got its hand stuck
And then there were two.

Two menacing Munchkins found a gun,
One shot his head off
And then there was one.

One menacing Munchkin never wanted to change
And that one menacing Munchkin said,
'It's time for revenge!'

Brandon Ibbotson (10)
Braidside Integrated Primary School, Ballymena

Ten Bouncy Footballs

(Inspired by 'Ten Little Schoolboys' by A A Milne)

Ten bouncy footballs flying over the line,
One got kicked away,
Then there were nine.

Nine bouncy footballs going directly straight,
One went in the wrong direction,
Then there were eight.

Eight bouncy footballs getting kicked by Kevin,
One went over,
Then there were seven.

Seven bouncy footballs all in a mix,
One got picked out,
Then there were six.

Six bouncy footballs getting kicked at a hive,
One got stung and burst,
Then there were five.

Five bouncy footballs outside a door,
Someone tripped over one,
Then there were four.

Four bouncy footballs, one belonged to me,
I took it away,
So then there were three.

Three bouncy footballs getting kicked by me and you,
Along came Peter,
Then there were two.

Two bouncy footballs sad because they were missing some,
One rolled away,
Then there was one.

One flat football used to think he was a hero,
Looks like he was wrong,
Then there were zero.

Ryan Gault (10)
Braidside Integrated Primary School, Ballymena

Ten Dancing Dinosaurs

(Inspired by 'Ten Little Schoolboys' by A A Milne)

Ten dancing dinosaurs in a chorus line,
One couldn't sing very loud,
And then there were nine.

Nine dancing dinosaurs all using bait,
One ate it himself,
And then there were eight.

Eight dancing dinosaurs making fun of Kevin,
One made fun of a T-rex,
And then there were seven.

Seven dancing dinosaurs were all trying tricks,
One went too far,
And then there were six.

Six dancing dinosaurs drinking 5-Alive,
One drank too much,
And then there were five.

Five dancing dinosaurs trying to reach the Earth's core,
One dug too much,
And then there were four.

Four dancing dinosaurs needing a pee,
One wet himself,
And then there were three.

Three dancing dinosaurs trying something new,
One broke his leg,
And then there were two.

Two dancing dinosaurs doing a run,
One tripped on a stone,
And then there was one.

One dancing dinosaur trying to be a hero,
He got carried away,
And then there were zero.

Zero dancing dinosaurs with nothing to do,
Because they have gone
Away from you.

Danny Bryson (10)
Braidside Integrated Primary School, Ballymena

Ten Cheeky Monkeys

(Inspired by 'Ten Little Schoolboys' by A A Milne)

Ten cheeky monkeys went down a mine,
One choked on coal
And then there were nine.

Nine cheeky monkeys went on a date,
One got her heart broken
And then there were eight.

Eight cheeky monkeys went to Heaven,
One was bad
And then there were seven.

Seven cheeky monkeys playing with sticks,
One snapped theirs
And then there were six.

Six cheeky monkeys drinking 5-Alive,
One got hyper,
Then there were five.

Five cheeky monkeys knocking at a door,
One got a splinter,
Then there were four.

Four cheeky monkeys couldn't see,
One turned the light on,
Then there were three.

Three cheeky monkeys went to the zoo,
One didn't come out,
Then there were two.

Two cheeky monkeys were eating a bun,
One ate it all,
Then there was one.

One sad monkey had no fun,
She walked home,
Then there were none.

Elizabeth Rose Rainey (11)
Braidside Integrated Primary School, Ballymena

Ten Loopy Leprechauns!

(Inspired by 'Ten Little Schoolboys' by A A Milne)

Ten loopy leprechauns disobeying a sign,
One walked off a cliff
And then there were nine.

Nine loopy leprechauns went on a date,
One got stood up
And then there were eight.

Eight loopy leprechauns beat up Kevin,
One met the dad
And *then* there were seven.

Seven loopy leprechauns threw some bricks,
One got hit
And then there were six.

Six loopy leprechauns looked in a hive,
One got stung
And then there were five.

Five loopy leprechauns rode a boar,
One fell off
And then there were four.

Four loopy leprechauns went out to sea,
One couldn't swim
And then there were three.

Three loopy leprechauns went to Timbuktu,
One got lost
And then there were two.

Two loopy leprechauns having fun,
One had too much
And then there was one.

One loopy leprechaun having no fun,
It jumped off a cliff
And then there were none.

Mark Clements (11)
Braidside Integrated Primary School, Ballymena

Ten Dancing Dinosaurs

(Inspired by 'Ten Little Schoolboys' by A A Milne)

Ten dancing dinosaurs in a chorus line,
One couldn't sing,
Then there were nine.

Nine dancing dinosaurs all had a date,
One got too worried,
Then there were eight.

Eight dancing dinosaurs went up to Heaven,
One got lost,
Then there were seven.

Seven dancing dinosaurs ate Weetabix,
One choked on it,
Then there were six.

Six dancing dinosaurs loved being alive,
One got overjoyed,
Then there were five.

Five dancing dinosaurs played knick-knock on a door,
One got caught,
Then there were four.

Four dancing dinosaurs climbed up a tree,
One fell down,
Then there were three.

Three dancing dinosaurs had to use the loo,
One got sucked in,
Then there were two.

Two dancing dinosaurs ate some buns,
One ate too much,
Then there was one.

One dancing dinosaur wasn't having any fun,
He went back home,
Then there were none.

Joshua McAdorey (11)
Braidside Integrated Primary School, Ballymena

Fun

Fun tastes like candy.
Fun looks like children.
Fun smells like doughnuts.
Fun sounds like screaming.
Fun feels like a bundle of wool.
Fun is the colours of the rainbow.
Fun reminds me of the fair!

Danielle Jackson (10)
Braidside Integrated Primary School, Ballymena

Mary's Black Lamb

Mary had a little lamb
Whose fleece was black as soot.
Everywhere that Mary went
Its sooty foot it put.

Mary went to school one day,
Laughing with the crowd,
And when her black lamb showed itself,
Mary felt quite proud.

Mary was off school one week,
For she had chickenpox,
Her little black lamb cheered her up
By playing with her socks.

Mary loved her lamb so much
She kept it in her sight,
But her lamb, it thought *I'll get out,*
I'll try with all my might.

But her lamb did not succeed,
He stayed there in captivity.
He tried and tried and thought to himself,
This is a hard activity!

Tillie Gray (11)
Broughshane Primary School, Broughshane

Rubbish

Rubbish, rubbish, all over the place,
Sometimes I wish it was as clean as space.
Rubbish, rubbish, all over the city,
I think it's a real pity.
Rubbish, rubbish, all over town,
All dirty and brown.
Rubbish, rubbish, in the street,
Oh what a mess for the man to sweep.
Rubbish, rubbish, that you produce,
Recycle, reuse, reduce.

Philip Kennedy (10)
Broughshane Primary School, Broughshane

The Little Seagull

See the little seagull,
Black and white,
See the little seagull
In its plight.

Hear the little seagull,
It hardly makes a sound,
Hear the little seagull
Moaning on the ground.

Touch the little seagull,
Its feathers covered in oil,
Touch the little seagull,
It makes your insides coil.

Smell the little seagull,
It smells just like the gutter,
Smell the little seagull,
It makes you cough and splutter.

David Craig (10)
Broughshane Primary School, Broughshane

My Teacher

My teacher, he is wonderful.
My teacher, he is great.
Sometimes I would even wish
He was my best mate.

He's loving, kind and caring,
Fun to be around.
When it comes around to work,
We can't make a sound.

He always has us laughing,
If we're not there's something wrong.
Sometimes when we're working,
He will start to sing a song.

I've had my share of teachers,
Still this one is the best.
He shares all his knowledge,
Also puts mine to the test.

Kerry-Ann Smyth (11)
Broughshane Primary School, Broughshane

Butterflies

Butterflies, butterflies, in the air,
Butterflies, butterflies, everywhere.

Butterflies, butterflies, flying around,
Butterflies, butterflies, make no sound.

Butterflies, butterflies, like flowers so bright,
Butterflies, butterflies, don't fly at night.

Butterflies, butterflies, are very small,
Butterflies, butterflies, God made them, one and all.

Matthew McNeill (11)
Broughshane Primary School, Broughshane

My Monster Sister

My monster sister,
She messes up my room,
She tells on me
And Mum always believes her.

My monster sister,
She makes me very cross,
She jumps on my bed and pulls my hair!

My monster sister,
She makes me do bad things
And Mum gets cross.

Emily, her name is cute,
We sometimes share special secrets,
Then I forget she's a monster
And we talk together . . .

Rebecca McAleese (10)
Broughshane Primary School, Broughshane

Hungry Snake

I am a very hungry snake,
Looking for food to stop my bellyache.

Slither, slither through the night,
Out to get myself a bite.

My senses tell me to climb this tree
And wait for my prey to come to me.

I smelt something with a flick of my tongue,
So down from my branch I silently swung.

That big fat rat didn't hear me come,
Now I've got him in my tum!

Adam McClintock (11)
Broughshane Primary School, Broughshane

Rubbish

Rubbish, rubbish, it's everywhere.
Rubbish, rubbish, no one cares.
Rubbish, rubbish, it pollutes the air.
Rubbish, rubbish, it's just not fair.

Rubbish, rubbish, why, I ask?
Putting it in the bin is not a hard task.
Rubbish, rubbish on the ground,
Rubbish, rubbish all around.

Rubbish, rubbish, recycle it,
It won't end up in a landfill pit.
Look after this world, keep it neat,
Don't increase the global heat.

Joshua McNabney (11)
Broughshane Primary School, Broughshane

What Happens At School

Sitting, watching, listening too,
All the things that we must do.
Homework, revision, it must be done,
To pass my test and have some fun.
Summer vacation, I can't wait
To get out of that old school gate.
All the work that we must do,
Isn't hard, nor easy too.
I like school in a way,
But at the end I shout hooray!
I miss my friends, I have to say,
But sometimes it's better just this way.

Shannon Beckett (11)
Broughshane Primary School, Broughshane

My School Teacher

My school teacher is so cool,
With her highland chestnut-coloured hair.

My school teacher is so cool,
Sitting in her chair.

My school teacher is so cool,
She makes me laugh every day.

My school teacher is so cool
In her own funny way.

My school teacher is so cool,
As thin as thin could be.

My school teacher is so cool,
She's the teacher for me.

Lauren Connor (10)
Broughshane Primary School, Broughshane

Friendship

Friendship is like traffic lights,
It always keeps on changing.
Try not to let it be a burden,
Like when it deserts you,
Like the dog that bites,
It really, really might,
Or it can be really, really nice,
Like sugar, not rice.
It's sometimes like a roller coaster,
But it's still full of love.
Just look and you should find it.
We are incomplete without it.

Cameron McNeill (9)
Broughshane Primary School, Broughshane

Winter

Snowdrops in winter,
A sign of snow,
See how they grow,
Fast or slow.

It's Christmas Day,
The snow falls,
I want to play,
So hip hip hooray!

Sophie Dennison (7)
Broughshane Primary School, Broughshane

Snowdrops

Snowdrops blossom in winter,
They look like snow,
Thin green steams
Grow from the ground.

Their droopy little heads
Have three white petals,
A long green stem,
I like snowdrops.

Robert Gordon (7)
Broughshane Primary School, Broughshane

Winter

Snowdrops in my garden,
See how they glow,
They look like snow.
My teacher likes snowdrops
And I like them too.

Erin Douglas (7)
Broughshane Primary School, Broughshane

Friendship

Friendship is something that is good and bad, but we all need it.
Sometimes friends use you and sometimes they help you.
It can be like a chocolate heart around you,
Or it can be pressure like a bossy person who is lonely and
needs a friend.
So you need to help him or her because everyone needs a friend.
Be helpful, be a friend to whoever needs it,
Because if you were lonely you would want a friend too.

Daniel Faith (8)
Broughshane Primary School, Broughshane

Friendship

Friendship is good,
Friendship is bad,
It is like a roller coaster,
It is like the colours of a rainbow,
We need it or else we will be lonely.
It's like a chocolate heart hugging you.

Thomas Ferguson (9)
Broughshane Primary School, Broughshane

Friendship

Friendship glows just like that,
Friendship makes the pain go back,
Friendship is as strong as steel,
Friendship makes everything go back down,
Friendship warms us like the sun,
It will take us to the end,
We all need friendship in the end.

Joel Adams (9)
Broughshane Primary School, Broughshane

Friendship

Friendship is like a roller coaster,
It is the colour of the rainbow.
Friendship is like a set of traffic lights.
Friendship is like a chocolate heart around you.
Friendship never lets you down.
Friendship is love.
Friendship glows like a burning fire.
Friendship tastes like sugar.
We all need friendship!

Philip Gregg (9)
Broughshane Primary School, Broughshane

Friendship

It is the colour of life,
It glows bright,
It tastes like cinnamon,
It is chocolate wrapped around you tight,
It makes your heart all warm,
It's hugs and kisses from me to you,
Look after it and it will look after you.

Susannah Graham (8)
Broughshane Primary School, Broughshane

Friendship

Friendship is a candle glowing bright,
Like the sun that warms us up.
It can be a bit bossy,
And it can be the dog that bites.
It can be the colour of the rainbow,
It can be love and happiness around you.
It can be a burden, friendship, but -
You never know what could happen.

David Stevenson (8)
Broughshane Primary School, Broughshane

Friendship

Friendship is happiness and love,
It is like the colours of a rainbow.
Friendship tastes like marshmallows,
It glows brightly around us.
Friendship is like a cuddly bear,
It is like a roller coaster.
Friendship is the sun warming us.
Friendship - we need it!

Claire Adams (9)
Broughshane Primary School, Broughshane

Two Silly Boys

John and Jack were silly boys,
They never stopped playing with toys.
Their favourite toy was a plane,
But it was left behind in Spain.
'They are so silly,' their mother said,
'All the junk food messes with their head,
But I still like them, yes I do,
Sometimes I can be silly too.'

Stuart Miller (11)
Broughshane Primary School, Broughshane

Friendship

Friendship can be good,
But friendship can be bad,
And friendship is the dog that bites,
But it can be harmless too.
So friendship is pretty much
Everything!
And . . . you can't live without it!

Shane Gibson (9)
Broughshane Primary School, Broughshane

Friendship

Friendship is like a roller coaster,
Bobbing up and down.
Sometimes it's like sugar,
All sweet and sound.
When you're feeling lonely
Or feeling upside down,
You know you don't have anybody,
It makes you want to frown.
But when you have a friend
Who makes everyone cheer,
You know you are the lucky one,
Because you know she's always here.

Emma Purdy (9)
Broughshane Primary School, Broughshane

Sounds

Sounds are all around us,
We hear them all the time,
From when the birds start cheeping
Until the church bells chime.

The footsteps in the alley,
Flicking on the light,
Reading us a story,
Mummy says, 'Goodnight.'

Pitter-patter of raindrops
Falling on the ground,
And think of all the wonders
Of every little sound!

Chloe Kernohan (10)
Broughshane Primary School, Broughshane

Friendship

What a moan,
What a drone,
Miss All High And Mighty.
The teacher is such a preacher,
But however bad she is,
She's a teacher and that's what she's for.
But you, my friend,
You're another story.
You are my friend,
You are there for me,
However mean I ever may be.
You are my friend,
I love you.

Sarah Eccles (9)
Broughshane Primary School, Broughshane

Friendship

Friendship is like a flower,
Big, beautiful and happy,
But sometimes it can be
Bossy, horrible and lonely.
Friendship is like a rainbow,
Colourful, bright and smiley.
Mostly it's a roller coaster,
You always get lost,
But you need friendship,
It will never let you down.

Kathleen Witherspoon (9)
Broughshane Primary School, Broughshane

Farming

Farming is a hard job,
Feeding all the animals,
Cows, sheep and the sheepdogs,
Driving the tractor with the trailer,
To the markets selling sheep,
Paying the bills for animal feed
And equipment too,
Drawing in the silage and hay.

But we see warm summer mornings
When the sun peeps behind the hedge,
Birds in tiny nests,
Baby animals being born,
Rain shining through the rainbow,
And beautiful nature all around me.

Aaron Smyrell (10)
Broughshane Primary School, Broughshane

Blue Is . . .

Blue is fresh
Cold blowing through my body,
Making cars blow over,
Blue is strong.

Blue is a deep blue wave
Crashing through the rocks,
Boats bobbing up and down,
Blue is beautiful.

Alyson Erwin (8)
Broughshane Primary School, Broughshane

I Wonder?

I wonder what would happen . . .
If I let a lion run about the house,
If I let go a mouse
If I let bees fly free,
Would they come after me?

I wonder what would happen . . .
If I had a scary nightmare,
If I had a rock star for a dad,
If I had long flowing hair,
It could blow in the air.

I wonder what would happen . . .
If the sun did not shine,
If the moon was made of cheese,
If my friends and I went
On adventures to mystical places.

Lois Cupples (11)
Broughshane Primary School, Broughshane

Friendship

It's like the colour of the rainbow,
It tastes of a chocolate heart,
It glows all the time,
It makes you feel all happy when you're down.
Friendship makes time go by,
It's as strong as steel,
It will always be there for you,
So long as you are there for it.

Jonathan Loughridge (9)
Broughshane Primary School, Broughshane

Nightmare

Nightmare sleeping in my bed,
Pulling the covers over my head.
Shadows creeping by my window,
Scary noises curl my toes.

Ghosties flying round my room,
What a spooky noise when they go *boom*.
Zombies thumping at my door,
Mice scratching at my floor.

Goblins rowing through the river,
Lying in my bed I quiver.
Witches flying up high,
I feel a twinkle in my right thigh.

But when I wake up in the morning,
When dawn is dawning,
Then I see the light.
I keep remembering last night.

Jade Lamont (9)
Broughshane Primary School, Broughshane

Friendship

Friendship is a roller coaster
Sitting on a mountain top.
You could be lonely,
But you should never stop
Looking for a good friend.
So keep looking and when the
Going gets tough, don't quit.
Give them some chocolate and say,
'Will you be my friend?'

Kara Taylor (9)
Broughshane Primary School, Broughshane

My Pet Lion

My pet lion
Is called Ryan,
He is big and furry,
People think he's scary,
When he eats a red berry.

My pet lion can talk,
He can walk,
He can dance,
He sings,
He can play dead.
My pet lion is so cool!

My pet lion likes to play football,
When he scores he does a weird dance!

Jordan McClean (10)
Broughshane Primary School, Broughshane

Friendship

It is the colour of a rainbow,
As flowing as the sea,
It makes you feel warm
Like the sun,
It's like a huge, big hug
The size of a tree,
It makes you feel all happy
And not alone,
It tastes like a honeybee
And it never, ever lets you down.

Rebecca Marcus (8)
Broughshane Primary School, Broughshane

My Teacher, Mrs H

Mrs H is . . .
Sweet and generous,
Caring and loving,
Kind and considerate,
She can also shout!

Mrs H looks like . . .
A supermodel!
She has brown-greyish hair,
Glasses and a scarf.
She loves chocolate!

Mrs H has . . .
A loving heart.
She makes me work for me,
I always try my best,
We respect each other.

Amy McAllister (10)
Broughshane Primary School, Broughshane

Who Is My Best Friend?

Who is my best friend?
She is kind, funny and always makes me happy
When I am sad and down.
We've been best friends since we've been in playschool,
And we will be best friends for life.
Now I know who my best friend is,
It's *Caitlin Lennon*.

Shannon Erwin (8)
Broughshane Primary School, Broughshane

Me

I am . . .
Tall and skinny
With ginger hair,
Freckles on my face,
With dark blue eyes.

I am . . .
Funny and silly,
Weird and wonderful,
Helpful and handy,
Kind and playful.

I am . . .
Happy and sad,
Good and bad,
Mannerly and cool,
Just a little too crazy!

Emma Heron (10)
Broughshane Primary School, Broughshane

My Dog

My dog is called Heidi,
She is a light brown and white,
But she won't bite.
She is usually crazy.

She chases my dad
But she will never hurt him.
I wish I could have five of them
But that will never happen.

Emily Erwin (7)
Broughshane Primary School, Broughshane

Colours

Blazing bright sun,
Deep blue sea,
Pretty petal pink,
They're the colours for me.

Lime-grass green,
Pure scarlet-red poppies,
Deep cream pearl,
These are the colours on my bed.

Pale, pure white, candyfloss clouds,
Dark, black, spooky nights,
Grey, sad winter days,
Then follow the pale blue skies of spring.

Megan Montgomery (10)
Broughshane Primary School, Broughshane

When I Feel Relaxed

When I feel relaxed it's like being a mermaid
With a shimmering tail that glistens in the water,
Like a fairy with a twinkle in its wing,
Like a godmother sharing a spell,
It's like a wave rolling in from the sea,
When a magical unicorn flies through the air,
It feels like I'm a princess with golden wavy hair.
I love it when I feel relaxed.

Nicole Turtle (9)
Broughshane Primary School, Broughshane

My Dog, Glen

My dog, Glen,
We play all day,
He likes to play his way,
He treats our yard like a den.

He likes to play football,
I always say,
We play every day,
He chews my sister's doll.

He plays with me,
We do lots of tricks
Beside the bricks,
Then Mum calls me in for tea.

Thomas Bell (11)
Broughshane Primary School, Broughshane

The Fledgling

Enter the nest . . .
It's a wonderful dark place,
Your new home, safe and secure,
Quiet and cosy.

Enter the nest . . .
You will make new friends,
Break your fragile shell
And creep into the light.

Alex Marshall (10)
Broughshane Primary School, Broughshane

My Puppy

My dog is fuzzy,
He's a cute little puppy,
He smells every day
Like a flower bouquet
That's starting to decay.

He's big and loving,
You know he's coming,
He will always be near,
Now he's here
It's time for fear,
Time to play with my cute little puppy.
I love my puppy, don't you?

Jonathan Cummings (10)
Broughshane Primary School, Broughshane

My Dream

My dream is to play for Liverpool,
Play midfield when I run up the pitch.
Their strip is the colour red,
Their sponsor is Carlsberg,
I feel proud.
The wind rushes past my face
As I run up the outside,
My heart pounds with excitement,
I pick up the pass and kick,
I hear the shouts,
It's a goal!

Steven Galloway (11)
Broughshane Primary School, Broughshane

Who Is My Best Friend?

She is different I know,
That is why I like her.
She met me at playschool
And she has never let me down.

She is happy and very clever,
She helps me when I'm down
And she never has a frown.
She got her mum to build my puzzle ball.

I now know who my best friend is,
It's Shannon Erwin!
We will be friends forever,
Past the end of time!

Caitlin Lennon (9)
Broughshane Primary School, Broughshane

My New Dog

My new dog is black and white,
She has blue eyes like me.
She likes to chase my hens
And the cows in the fields.

She helps my dad do some work,
I take her for a walk,
She follows me when I call her,
I love her very much.

She runs very fast and jumps up on me,
I love her and she is very good.
I love giving her doggy biscuits
And taking her for walks as well.

Grace McNeill (8)
Broughshane Primary School, Broughshane

Red Is . . .

Red is spooky and spinny,
Walking through a tunnel,
Bats flying around,
Big red eyes.
I was walking
Through and through,
I was getting really scared.

Jessica Newell (8)
Broughshane Primary School, Broughshane

Monsters

Monsters
Chasing me
Down the road
But it's only my
Shadow.

Spiders
Crawling up
The old wall,
Crawling back down again.
Argh!

Andrew McKee (8)
Broughshane Primary School, Broughshane

Winter

W e love to play in the snow
I love the cold feeling of the snow
N early every year it comes
T oday I will be getting presents
E arly in the day I'll wake up, what's under the tree?
R ight, who's taken my presents? They were for me!

Courtney Lewis (8)
Broughshane Primary School, Broughshane

My New Dog

My dog is cute, my dog is sweet,
My dog is loveable and he's adorable.

He's only new so he runs away
And it's hard to catch him 'cause he runs very fast.

He's a Lakeland Terrier and his name is buster.
He's got wiry hair so he's very fuzzy.

Susie Neeson (7)
Broughshane Primary School, Broughshane

Animals

A nimals are different
N aughty animals, clever animals
I love them all
M aybe a lion could bite you
A nimals are different
L ittle ones, big ones
S cary animals, but I still love every one of them.

Caitlin Caldwell (9)
Broughshane Primary School, Broughshane

My Dad

My daddy loves Liverpool,
He has Liverpool number plates,
He is mad about Liverpool
And he shouts 'Yeah' when they score a goal.

My dad gets me football cards,
I have got a couple of Liverpool ones.
My daddy's favourite player
Is Steven Gerrard.

Morgen Blair (7)
Broughshane Primary School, Broughshane

Summer Is . . .

Summer is . . .
Like a lovely summery colour,
Gold, yellow, red and blue.

Summer is . . .
Like a fabulous sunshine
In the fade of blue.

Summer is . . .
Like a pot of gold,
My favourite season of the year.

Summer is . . .
Like going on holidays to the gold sand.
Shivering when I'm in the cold sea.

Naomi Crawford (8)
Broughshane Primary School, Broughshane

Red Is . . .

Red is hot, fiery lava,
Like the sun
Burning you up like nothing,
Like two hot, fiery hands
Throwing you into the fire,
As if you're a bit of toast
About to be burnt,
Like you're a sausage
Frying in a pan,
About to be eaten,
Like a sparkler about to burn you.

Laura Craig (7)
Broughshane Primary School, Broughshane

Trees

People like trees,
It's lovely in the breeze.
Trees make their own food,
It's very, very good.
Leaves blow in the breeze
In every degree.

Trees give us wood
And all sorts of food.
They give us shade from the sun,
When we are having fun,
Especially in the sun.
The trees touch the sky,
They're really, really high.

The tree is covered in green,
It's a lovely sight to be seen.
The tree looks gold,
Even though it's old,
And in the spring
Fresh green leaves are what it will bring.

Paige Murray (10)
Buick Memorial Primary School, Cullybackey

Summer

Summer is orange and blue.
It tastes like strawberry ice cream,
It sounds like a sizzling barbecue,
It looks like a garden full of flowers and butterflies,
It smells like the sand,
It makes me feel hot.

Katie Farquhar (8)
Buick Memorial Primary School, Cullybackey

World War II

Bombs, gunshots,
Screaming, crying,
They thought war had ended
Years ago.

But now they know they're wrong.
Children getting on trains,
Your parents might go to war,
Then maybe not come back.

Planes crashing down,
Crying, dying, then silence.
This was the tragedy of
World War II.

Beth Orr (9)
Buick Memorial Primary School, Cullybackey

I'm A Cheetah

I am a cheetah,
I love to cheat a lot.
When I run fast,
I can get very hot.
When I'm in the desert,
I lie in the shade.
I don't eat chocolate
But I drink lemonade.

Shannon Burnside (8)
Buick Memorial Primary School, Cullybackey

My Classroom

Computer screen blinking,
While children are thinking.
Artistic displays on the walls around,
And the clock hands moving without a sound.

The sound of children reading,
Their busy pencils softly writing.
Chairs are scraping on the floor,
In the corner, two boys fighting.

I'm happy to be in this class 'cause
It gets my brain going bright,
Concentrating on my work,
Thinking if I can get it right.

Ross Evans (8)
Buick Memorial Primary School, Cullybackey

Volcano

V olcanoes are bad and dangerous
O n top of the volcano there is a hole
L ava is hot, it is red and orange
C olour of the volcano is grey
A volcano is very big
N ow these days volcanoes are knocked down
O ften every volcano explodes.

Josh Weir (8)
Buick Memorial Primary School, Cullybackey

Volcanoes

V olcanoes are extremely dangerous
O nce a volcano took over a city
L ava and lightning can be dangerous
C racks are all over volcanoes
A volcano can kill you and others
N o volcanoes will explode here
O ften volcanoes have super, super hot powers
E xplosive volcanoes splash hard and kill you
S ome volcanoes don't work anymore.

Adam Taggart (8)
Buick Memorial Primary School, Cullybackey

I'm A Pterodactyl

I'm a pterodactyl,
I think flying is fun,
I run all day
And then I eat a bun.

I'm a pterodactyl,
I've got wings,
You won't touch me
Because I've got rings.

I'm a pterodactyl,
I'm not fat,
I'm very skinny,
And that is that!

James Kennedy (7)
Buick Memorial Primary School, Cullybackey

My Dog

My dog is brown and white
With fluffy ears, just what I like.

I love to take it for a walk
And as we stroll I speak doggy talk.

One day we gave her a shampoo bath,
But she took off down the garden path.

Across the lawn into the vegetable patch,
She tossed and turned and began to scratch.

The weeds and clay flew into the air
And what was clean now was dirt everywhere.

Philip Fenton (10)
Buick Memorial Primary School, Cullybackey

Snakes

The snake is very scaly,
The snake is very big,
The snake is very tall,
The snake can eat a pig!

I'm a snake, I am very weird,
I'm a snake on the plain.
I'm a snake, I will shed my skin,
I'm a snake and I will eat the lion's mane.

Thomas McMurray (7)
Buick Memorial Primary School, Cullybackey

The Clever Cat

I've got a cat, he is as clever as a fox.
He has special abilities, he can escape from any box.
When he is asleep he is dreaming of fish for his tea.
He can open my door using a key!
He always has a plan up his paws,
You'd better watch out, he'll eat you raw!

Sam Hutchinson (8)
Buick Memorial Primary School, Cullybackey

My Cat, Mack

Mack, my cat, is very lazy,
He has a girlfriend called Maisie.
Maisie is the opposite of Mack,
She is always on the go,
She is the quick one - Mack is so slow.
I love my cat Mack,
Even though he is a pest,
But to me, my Mack is the *best!*

Ellen Harkness (8)
Buick Memorial Primary School, Cullybackey

My Dream

The night is dark, I cannot see,
I have not brought my specs with me.
I'm in a park, a twig, it snaps,
And something flits across the path.
I run, I stumble and fall.
I wake up in my bed,
I've had a nightmare.

Emily Keys (10)
Buick Memorial Primary School, Cullybackey

Sweep, The Cat

Sweep, my cat, is brown all over,
He is silently sleeping through the day,
But he hunts at night,
He looks for things to eat.
In his cosy box he sighs!
I love my cat Sweep, although he's a pest,
But I think he is brilliant!

Hannah Cooke (8)
Buick Memorial Primary School, Cullybackey

Summer

Summer is bright yellow and dark red.
It tastes like ice lollies and cold drinks,
It sounds like children shouting in the sea,
It looks like children having fun,
It smells like the new grass growing,
It makes me feel warm and free.

Georga Gordon (8)
Buick Memorial Primary School, Cullybackey

School

Every day
I like to play,
I don't like boys
Who make a noise.
English, maths, PE, art,
Asking questions, taking part.
I love to be at school
And do not like to break a rule.

Lois McCurdy (9)
Buick Memorial Primary School, Cullybackey

My Little Sister

Big blue eyes,
Four small teeth,
Fine brown hair
And rosy-red cheeks.

She says, 'Ma-ma' and 'Da-da,'
Cries in her cot,
Shouts for her bottle,
And when I tickle, she giggles a lot.

I'm happy when she's peaceful,
It's fun when she laughs at me,
I'm sad when her gums are sore,
I'm as proud of her as I can be.

Katie Adams (9)
Buick Memorial Primary School, Cullybackey

Ice Skating

Curving scratches on the glittering ice,
Skating tutors teaching wonderful spins,
Scared people grabbing tightly on the rails,
Ice dancers practising their routines.

My blades scrape across the ice,
Playful skaters laugh and shout,
Cries of 'Help!' from worried beginners,
People shrieking when they fall about.

Experienced skaters whizzing past,
Enjoyment flows around the hall,
I'm thrilled when I do something well,
Though my heart is pounding in case I fall.

Hannah Wylie (9)
Buick Memorial Primary School, Cullybackey

My Silly Guinea Pig

He has a really big, fat body,
Messy and covered with sawdust,
Small pink ears on his whiskery face,
Beautiful, clean, white hair when he's brushed.

Slurping water out of his water bottle,
He plays on a ball with a bell,
He squeaks when you shake a bag
And snuffles in the sawdust as well.

I feel joy when I see him and hold him,
Watch out for his sharp white teeth!
When I stroke his soft brown and white hair,
I feel his sharp claws underneath.

Simone Lyle (9)
Buick Memorial Primary School, Cullybackey

My Mountain Bike

A dirty bike which I'm going to ride,
An old broken bell nearly rusted away,
A blue frame with a splash of red here and there,
But a seat so soft I could sit on it all day.

The chains clank as I change gear,
My bell rings as I whizz past.
Stones fly off things when I brake,
And the tyres squeal as I corner fast.

I feel as if I'm a professional,
Happy, entertained by the things all around,
Flying like I'm out of control,
Scared in case I fall off and hit the ground.

Adam McCallion (9)
Buick Memorial Primary School, Cullybackey

Dinosaurs

I like to play outside.
My dinosaur likes to play with me.
My dinosaur and I like to play on our bikes.
My dinosaur and I like to look at the sea.

I am a stegosaurus,
I am bad.
I make my dad mad,
My dad gets mad.

I am an anklyosaurus,
I am bad,
I make my dad mad,
I make my mum mad.

Curtis Wylie (7)
Buick Memorial Primary School, Cullybackey

My Bedroom

I like my high wooden bed,
Pink painted walls all around,
My TV on the wall
And my toys on the ground.

The dehumidifier humming,
All my family soundly sleeping,
My room is usually peaceful
Until my morning alarm starts beeping.

When I'm tired at night I love my bed,
When things go wrong, it's a place to be sad,
And I feel calm, alone in my room,
It's my perfect place, I'm so glad.

Courtney McFetridge (9)
Buick Memorial Primary School, Cullybackey

School

May I play
With your toy today?
No way,
Go away.
I was sad,
This boy was bad.
I kicked the ball
Against the wall,
I only wanted to have fun,
To play with him and run.

Jack Dixon (8)
Buick Memorial Primary School, Cullybackey

My Ma's Running Machine

My ma just loves
Her running machine,
She's on it every day.

She walks a while,
She runs a while,
Trying hard to do
Four miles.

She puts it up,
She puts it down,
All the time
Trying hard to shed
A few pounds.

My dad, he says
It's a waste of time,
But nothing changes
My ma's mind.

Melissa Graham (9)
Buick Memorial Primary School, Cullybackey

Sleep

Sleep is peaceful,
Sleep is brill,
Sleep is pure silence,
It is just completely still.

Sleep is cool,
Sleep is great,
Sleep tastes like chocolate
Which I do not hate.

Sleep is something everyone does,
Sleep feels like pure silk,
Sleep is absolutely fabulous.

Susannah Kyle (10)
Buick Memorial Primary School, Cullybackey

Summer

School is out,
Children shout,
Summer's here,
Far and near.
Everyone can play
Every day,
Come on, let's go,
Don't be too slow.

Samuel Craig (9)
Buick Memorial Primary School, Cullybackey

The Oak Tree

The lovely oak tree standing tall,
Where animals play, big and small.
Bugs and birds live in this tree,
Squirrels and insects, hard to see.

Gemma Reid (9)
Buick Memorial Primary School, Cullybackey

Volcano

V olcanoes are dangerous
O nce upon a time, Slemish was a volcano
L ots of lava comes out
C areful, they are dangerous
A ll are dangerous and noisy
N oisy to watch but take care
O n the day Slemish erupted, you'd have been scared if
standing beside it!

Rachel McKay (8)
Buick Memorial Primary School, Cullybackey

Trees

Some trees are tall,
Some are small,
Buzzing bees
In the trees.
Why do people chop them down?
Trees in the country,
Trees in the town.
Food like apples, plums or pears,
Trees are home for squirrels or hares.

Ben Alexander Eaton (9)
Buick Memorial Primary School, Cullybackey

Sun

Sun is fun,
I'm ready to run
In the summer breeze,
Running through the trees.
I like the sun
Because it's fun.

Sophie Ervine (9)
Buick Memorial Primary School, Cullybackey

Volcano

V olcanoes are very dangerous and hot
O ut of the volcanoes lava comes down the mountain
L ava can kill people and turn them to stone
C ome on, the volcano has erupted and the volcano, it booms fire
A tree burns down and it is bad
N ot good when it happens
O h the silly volcano!

Jack Meneely (8)
Buick Memorial Primary School, Cullybackey

Summer

Summer is bright yellow sun and light blue sky.
It tastes like ice cream and ice lollies,
It sounds like shouting children running out of school,
It looks like children shouting in the sea,
It smells like the seaweed on the beach,
It makes me feel hot and happy.

Ashley Johnston (8)
Buick Memorial Primary School, Cullybackey

My Family

My mum is a cook,
My dad likes to look.
My nana spoils me a lot,
My grandad says I am the best he's got.

Chelsea Boyd (8)
Buick Memorial Primary School, Cullybackey

Spring

Spring is bright green and dark brown,
It tastes like chocolate eggs and warm pancakes,
It sounds like birds tweeting in the morning,
It looks like lambs running in the fields,
It smells like lovely flowers,
It makes me feel warm and safe.

Robert Adair (8)
Buick Memorial Primary School, Cullybackey

Summer

Summer is dark orange and bright red.
It tastes like the deep blue sea,
It sounds like waves in the sea,
It looks like the bright sun,
It smells like roses and poppies,
It makes me happy and lovely.

Joshua Galloway (7)
Buick Memorial Primary School, Cullybackey

T-rex

A *T*-rex eats dinosaurs.
They *R*un very fast
*E*at meat a lot
Bones are *X*-rayed when found.

Zak Humphrey (7)
Buick Memorial Primary School, Cullybackey

Happiness

Happiness is rainbow-coloured like festive flags.
It sounds like festival music,
It tastes like chocolate strawberries,
It looks like people smiling,
It feels like soft wool,
It reminds me of 'Daddy Day Camp.'

Rebecca Arbuthnot (9)
Buick Memorial Primary School, Cullybackey

Laughter

Laughter is yellow like Goldilocks' hair.
It sounds like a melody from the air,
It tastes like a bubble to my throat,
It looks like a bumpy car on the road,
It feels like a tickly vibration in my hand,
It reminds me of 'You've Been Framed'.

Bethany Brown (10)
Buick Memorial Primary School, Cullybackey

Sadness

Sadness is blue like dolphins.
It sounds like a puppy's whimper,
It tastes like saltwater,
It looks like aching eyes,
It feels like a wet finger,
It reminds me of the film 'Lost in the Forest'.

Cathy Reid (10)
Buick Memorial Primary School, Cullybackey

Happiness

Happiness is peachy-pink like festive flags.
It sounds like people laughing,
It tastes like iced buns,
It looks like people smiling,
It feels like soft woolly jumpers,
It reminds me of when my cousin was born!

Catherine McMillan (10)
Buick Memorial Primary School, Cullybackey

Hunger

Hunger is red like ribs.
It sounds like a tummy rumbling,
It tastes like thin broth,
It looks like a bony skeleton,
It feels like a dry mouth,
It reminds me of starving children in Africa.

Robbie Kelly (9)
Buick Memorial Primary School, Cullybackey

Silence

Silence is white, it is like falling snow.
It sounds like tiny footsteps pitter-pattering,
It tastes like vanilla ice cream,
It looks like an empty room,
It feels like fog,
It reminds me of 'Silence of the Lambs'.

Emma McDowell (10)
Buick Memorial Primary School, Cullybackey

Hate

Hate is blue like a storm.
It sounds like screams,
It tastes like the salty sea,
It looks like a devil,
It feels like steel knives,
It reminds me of 'Buffy the Vampire Slayer'.

Sarah Greer (10)
Buick Memorial Primary School, Cullybackey

Laughter

Laughter is yellow like the sun.
It sounds like a giggle to my ear,
It tastes like a bubble on my tongue,
It looks like a sweet daffodil,
It feels like a bubble bath,
It reminds me of cheese
And 'Home Alone'.

Lauren Neilly (9)
Buick Memorial Primary School, Cullybackey

Hate

Hate is red like blood.
It sounds like wolves howling,
It tastes like hot chilli peppers,
It looks like a roaring fire,
It feels like sharp knives,
It reminds me of 'Scream'.

Lydia Simpson (9)
Buick Memorial Primary School, Cullybackey

My Cat, Sam

I have a cat, his name is Sam,
He is a human garbage can!
He eats our food,
Which is no good,
He made a mess, my mum was cross,
She threw him out into the moss!
I came out with him,
Even though he made such a din!
I love Sam, my cat - he's really great,
I would never swap him, he's my best mate!

Jacob Knipe (7)
Buick Memorial Primary School, Cullybackey

Summer

Summer is bright yellow and dark orange.
It tastes like oranges and pears,
It sounds like children playing at the beach,
It looks like the bright sun shining over me,
It smells like ice cream and ice lollies,
It makes me feel happy and warm in the sun.

Amy Matthews (8)
Buick Memorial Primary School, Cullybackey

Anger

Anger is red like blood.
It sounds like a withering cry,
It tastes like curry,
It looks like a punch bag,
It feels like a burning furnace,
It reminds me of 'Hot Fuzz'.

Dion Houston (10)
Buick Memorial Primary School, Cullybackey

Tom, The Cat

Tom, the cat, is sneaky as a spy,
He sleeps in his basket and doesn't cry.
He naps all day on my bed,
He eats fish and cries until he is fed!
He gets stuck on the roof and can't get down,
He is the sneakiest cat around our town!

Alan Arbuthnot (8)
Buick Memorial Primary School, Cullybackey

McCavity, The Ginger Cat

McCavity is a ginger cat,
His fur is full of tats,
It is sleek and a beautiful shade,
He sleeps in a basket that I made!
He thinks it is nice
To be out catching mice!

Rebecca Allen (8)
Buick Memorial Primary School, Cullybackey

Tom, The Cat

My cat is black,
My cat's eyes are blue,
I like stew and he does too!
He likes me and I like him too,
But he hasn't a clue!
He's sometimes a pest,
But to me, he's simply the best!

Stuart MacGregor (8)
Buick Memorial Primary School, Cullybackey

Bumpy, The Cat

My cat is called Bumpy,
His tail is fat and lumpy.
His fur is pure black,
He loves to sleep in a sack!
He hunts for mice and rats,
He fights with other cats.
I love my cat Bumpy with all my heart,
Even though he's naughty and rips things apart!

Grace McCready (8)
Buick Memorial Primary School, Cullybackey

Bull, The Cat

Bull is my cat, he is white,
He trains all day, he hunts at night.
He hunts for food, he hunts for toys,
Then he sleeps and makes no noise!
He's vicious, he fights, he is a bit of a pest,
But to me he is simply the best.

Dylan Knipe (7)
Buick Memorial Primary School, Cullybackey

Soot, The Cat

I have a cat called Soot,
He never stays where he is put!
Sometimes he can be a pest,
He sneaks around without a rest.
Soot can cause a lot of bother
But I wouldn't change him for another!

Harry Gaston (8)
Buick Memorial Primary School, Cullybackey

Buster, The Cat

Buster the cat is lovely and black,
He sleeps in the garden on his back.
He loves to be violent,
Although he's very silent.
At night he sneaks out of the house
And always pounces on a mouse.
But when night becomes day,
He still wants to hunt for even more prey!

Charlie Neal (8)
Buick Memorial Primary School, Cullybackey

Zak, The Cat

My cat's name is Zak,
He's white and black.
He sleeps all day on top of the mat,
He hunts at night and climbs the fence!
I love my cat, I think he's fat!
I would never swap Zak for another cat!

Martin Dempsey (8)
Buick Memorial Primary School, Cullybackey

Mog, The Cat

My cat is called Mog,
He wants to be a dog!
When he gets no food
He's in a very bad mood!
Even though he's very mad,
He's great company and a good lad.

Isaac Simpson (7)
Buick Memorial Primary School, Cullybackey

Schwartz And Coal

Schwartz and Coal live at 2 Downel Heights.
Coal hunts at night with a friend who's white.
Don't annoy Schwartz or he'll give you a bite!
My brother thinks they're vicious,
But they think his food is delicious.
They make a mess, my mum gets cross,
But Schwartz doesn't care - he is the boss!

David Leetch (8)
Buick Memorial Primary School, Cullybackey

Jerry, The Mad Cat

Jerry is a fat cat,
He goes out hunting at night with the boys.
He is black and shiny,
He is fast on his feet,
He comes to my kitchen when he wants to eat.
He plays with a ball and it rolls around,
When he goes to bed, he makes no sound!

Zach Wilson (7)
Buick Memorial Primary School, Cullybackey

Sasha, The Cat

Sasha, my cat, is such a pest,
She tries to annoy us the very best,
But at night she is silent!
To other cats she is violent!
Sasha is the cat I love the most,
She sleeps all day on our garden post!

Harry Kenneway (7)
Buick Memorial Primary School, Cullybackey

Strawberry, The Cat

Strawberry, Strawberry, there is no one like her,
She sleeps anywhere, in the basement, or on my chair!
She is so good and clever at night,
She is sneaky,
But sometimes she is so loud I can't get to sleep.
She tries her best.
I love my cat Strawberry, she is so good.

Corrie Reid (7)
Buick Memorial Primary School, Cullybackey

Love

Love is pink like a heart.
Love is rose-pink like a beautiful flower.
It sounds like romantic music,
It tastes like delicious chocolates,
It looks like a diamond ring,
It feels like the first blossom of spring.
'Romeo and Juliet'.

Grace Henry (9)
Buick Memorial Primary School, Cullybackey

Fun

It sounds like Alton Towers,
It tastes like gummy bears,
It looks like SpongeBob,
It feels like a bouncy castle.
'Daddy Daycare'.
Fun is red like a Liverpool top.

Adam Mairs (10)
Buick Memorial Primary School, Cullybackey

My Dinosaur

I have a dinosaur,
He likes to give a roar,
But when he sees a bird,
He might fall to the floor!

I have a dinosaur,
He watches birds soar,
But he fixed my homework
Which he tore!

I have a dinosaur,
He is big and fat,
He is bigger than my house
Because I live in a flat!

Daniel Buick (7)
Buick Memorial Primary School, Cullybackey

Fun

Fun is blue like Barry's in Portrush.
It sounds like children playing,
It tastes like candyfloss,
It looks like a carnival,
It feels like you are up high in the big wheel.
'Daddy Day Care'.

James Simpson (9)
Buick Memorial Primary School, Cullybackey

Silence

Silence is white like snow falling.
It sounds like midnight,
It tastes like vanilla ice cream,
It looks like a slimy snail slithering along,
It feels like a mist,
It reminds me of 'Silence of the Lambs'.

Leah Harkin (10)
Buick Memorial Primary School, Cullybackey

The Three Wise Women

When the three wise men left by camel,
They left three wise women.
One said, 'He took gold for baby Jesus -
Just one hour old!'

'Mine took frankincense,'
Said the second.
'Men have no common sense!'

'And my man took myrrh,
So the baby smells doubly sweet,
Yes sir!'

Being worldly wise,
The wives made tiny
Nappies to his size.

Gifts he needed most,
And packaged them to him
By express post.

Alistair Givens (11)
Buick Memorial Primary School, Cullybackey

Ten New Year's Resolutions

To do my homework neatly - then feed it to the dog,
To be good all year round, except when I want to be bad,
Use my brain in class - think about home time!
To stop biting my fingernails - bite my thumbnails instead.
To be nice to my sister on weekdays - until half-past three.
To stop asking my parents for money - ask Granny instead.
To keep my music down - use headphones.
To get up at 7am when I'm going somewhere.
To stop spending money on crisps - buy sweets instead.
To scrap these resolutions without hesitation.

Amy Swann (10)
Buick Memorial Primary School, Cullybackey

Boats

When I get near to the lake
I see . . .
Boats turning gently,
Men fishing freely,
Bins overflowing,
The tide coming in.

When I reach the lake
I hear . . .
Fish splish-splashing,
Engines starting up,
Water skiers thumping,
Rubber dinghies bumping.

When I stand at the lake
I smell . . .
Smoke puffing out
Diesel fumes from tanks,
Fish being loaded,
Food being cooked.

Moses Kirk (8)
Buick Memorial Primary School, Cullybackey

Creation Of Dreamtime

The dreamtime world is full of
The sweet, joyful, constant singing of the birds,
The cold, crisp, white, snowy mountains,
The wind howling back to voices and of their ancestors,
The ever-changing colour of Uluru,
The shimmering of the tops of the lakes,
The shining stars that climb so high,
The soothing lullaby of the wind,
The sand's heat that feels great on your feet,
The colourful, decorated boomerang,
The colour of the beautiful night sky.

Ben Gaston (11)
Buick Memorial Primary School, Cullybackey

Dreamtime World

The dreamtime world is full of
The rustling of roses,
The whistling of the wind,
The calm, quiet and beautiful lakes,
The climbing koalas,
The brightness of the moon,
The silky feeling of a spider's web,
The fresh, luscious fruit,
The class colours of the rainbow,
The clean fur of a kangaroo,
The amazing sounds of a didgeridoo,
The salty water of Lake Eyre,
The extreme climate from the sun,
The breathtaking, colour-changing Uluru,
The power of the boomerang,
The sheep bouncing in the field,
The length of the Murray River.

Jordan Campbell (11)
Buick Memorial Primary School, Cullybackey

Ten New Year's Resolutions

To go to bed early - to play my PSP.
To visit Gran - on her shopping day.
To do my work - occasionally.
To do my reading, but not in the evening.
To not watch TV all the time - just most of the time.
To take the rubbish out - after the binman has been.
To read magazines - only if they are about tractors.
To tidy my bedroom - except on Saturdays.
To not fight with my brothers - every other week.
To scrap these resolutions without hesitation.

Adam McAuley (10)
Buick Memorial Primary School, Cullybackey

My Modern Twelve Days Of Christmas

On the twelfth day of Christmas . . .
Twelve candles glowing,
Eleven cards a-standing,
Ten reindeer flying,
Nine baubles hanging,
Eight stars a-shining,
Seven coloured stockings,
Six Christmas crackers,
Five springer spaniels,
Four skaters skating,
Three fat turkeys,
Two DVDs
And an Xbox 360.

Nicola Anderson (11)
Buick Memorial Primary School, Cullybackey

Aboriginal Dreamtime

The dreamtime world is full of
The beautifully grown coral, drifting in the reef,
The proud structure of Uluru standing tall,
The sandy deserts, scorched by the sun,
The majestic birds cutting through the air,
The bright blue sky illuminating the land,
The whisper of the ancestors piercing the fabric of the plains,
The brilliant cave paintings telling their artists' stories,
The silent flow of the Great Barrier Reef, protecting the marine life,
The whistle of a boomerang soaring past my head.

Stuart Wylie (11)
Buick Memorial Primary School, Cullybackey

Creation of Dreamtime

The dreamtime world is full of
The blowing of the grass,
The chirping of the birds,
The glistening of the stars,
The glance of the sun shining,
The ever-changing colour of Uluru,
The silence of the desert's sand,
The rustling of leaves in trees,
The cold breeze of the snow,
The mirage in the yellow desert,
The rhythm of the didgeridoo
And the sparking sound of the fires at night.

Samuel Beattie (11)
Buick Memorial Primary School, Cullybackey

Ten New Year's Resolutions

To not eat a lot of chocolate - when I'm sick.
To play with my friends - when they have money.
To be good for my mum - once a year.
To help everyone - only on their birthday.
To not talk in class - to shout in class.
To respect my elders - just to get something.
To be kind to Miss Q - when I can't see her.
To save my birthday money - after I spend it.
To help my mum with the shopping - when it is put away.
To scrap these resolutions - without hesitation.

Sam Sloan (11)
Buick Memorial Primary School, Cullybackey

Ten New Year Resolutions

To go to bed on time - and play the PS2.
To go to my granny's - on her shopping day.
To go back to school - on the wrong day.
To take the bin out - when the binman has been.
To listen to my mum - on the phone.
To go to a friend's house - when they have gone out.
To do my homework on the bus.
To bring an enemy to my house and put a pie in his face.
To bring a guest in and then kick him out.
To scrap these resolutions without hesitation.

Daniel Stephen Brown (11)
Buick Memorial Primary School, Cullybackey

Dreamtime World

The dreamtime world is full of
The song of the pukeko drifting through the air,
The brightness of the night sky,
The changing colours of the great Urulu,
The beauty of the life-full flowers,
The glistening sparkles of the lake,
The birth of a baby kangaroo,
The soft feeling of the snow on the mountains,
The large bird spreading its wonderful wings,
The helpful stars in the night sky.

Leoni Jean McQuilkin (11)
Buick Memorial Primary School, Cullybackey

Spell Of Sinister Evil

(Inspired by 'Macbeth')

'Double, double, toil and trouble,
Fire burn and cauldron bubble.'

Very big toad heads, three in one,
We killed them with a shotgun.

Now we add some special beer
So he doesn't know how to steer.

Now we needs some grass fungus,
It smells so humongous.

It's time to add some slimy goo,
The stuff that will give you the flu.

We have nearly got the mix,
Time to make a smell that sticks.

The cauldron starts to spit up fire,
As we have the most gruesome desires.

'Double, double, toil and trouble,
Fire burn and cauldron bubble.'

Robbie Campbell (11)
Buick Memorial Primary School, Cullybackey

Creation Of DreamTime

The dreamtime world is full of
The bright shining sun,
The big, silent, yellow desert,
The giant monolith of Uluru,
The wild whistling of the wind,
The swishing and booming of waves,
The twinkling of the stars,
The big, tall, snowy mountains,
And the sweet singing of the birds.

Luke Simpson (11)
Buick Memorial Primary School, Cullybackey

My Witches' Spell

(Inspired by 'Macbeth')

'Double, double, toil and trouble,
Fire burn and cauldron bubble.'

We will meet with Macbeth to scare,
No one could tell him to beware!

To invite King Duncan to kill,
The event will give him a chill.

He will regret and start to hagar,
Did the deed with his dreadful dagger.

Now he sits on the royal throne,
Suddenly he feels so alone.

Now Macbeth will have to confess,
Our plan is working, he is distressed!

To top this with beautiful bugs,
Look in dark, damp places for slugs.

A few dragon eyes to savour,
Help Macbeth with some *hard* labour.

'Double, double, toil and trouble,
Fire burn and cauldron bubble.'

Timothy Spence (11)
Buick Memorial Primary School, Cullybackey

My Cat Is Called Daisy

Daisy is a pedigree cat,
She sleeps all night on her mat.
My cat is all black and white,
She hunts sneakily at night.
She always win prizes,
She competes against cats all shapes and sizes!
My cat is the best cat in the world to me,
Even when she's naughty as can be!

Suzanne Reid (8)
Buick Memorial Primary School, Cullybackey

My Witches' Spell

(Inspired by 'Macbeth')

'Double, double, toil and trouble,
Fire burn and cauldron bubble.'

Now let's start this atrocious beat
While the cauldron picks up the heat.

Let's throw in a pile full of fleas,
These things are revolting to see.

From a fox we took eighteen hairs,
This is for the fiend that shall dare.

Take the bunions of some old folk,
This will surely make you choke.

Let's put in some rotten old bones,
With that you'll want to run home.

Then the person who tastes this plate
Will realise their awful fate.

'Double, double, toil and trouble,
Fire burn and cauldron bubble.'

Rhianna Campbell (10)
Buick Memorial Primary School, Cullybackey

Welcome To My Dreamtime

The dreamtime world is full of
The softness of the sand,
The whistling of the wind,
The frosty, chilly mountains,
The ripening of the plants,
The brightness of the sunset,
The singing of the birds,
The taste of the sweet and sour fruits,
The darkness of the caves
And a never-ending stream.

Rebecca Speers (10)
Buick Memorial Primary School, Cullybackey

Ten New Year's Resolutions

To hoover my room - every month.
To get up on time - on a Saturday.
To be nice to my sister - every other week.
To not start fights in the playground - every other week.
To not eat as much chocolate and greasy stuff - if I don't want to.
To not watch any TV and get more exercise - when the soaps
aren't on.
To improve my English - if the dog doesn't eat it.
To eat more healthy foods - every Sunday.
To scrap these resolutions without hesitation.

Alan Casey (11)
Buick Memorial Primary School, Cullybackey

Ten New Year's Resolutions

Not to annoy my brother - until he's asleep.
Go to bed on time - when I'm tired.
Practise my drumming - when my dad's asleep.
Feed my fish - when they're dead.
Tidy my room - every leap year.
Get out of bed on time - when I feel like it.
Do my homework - when I'm bored.
Not to annoy my sister - except when she's on the phone.
Do my reading - if there isn't a match on TV.
To scrap these resolutions without hesitation.

Gareth Evans (10)
Buick Memorial Primary School, Cullybackey

My Mum's Ring

Shines when she sits
In the sun by the window.

Spinning round on
My tiny little fingers.

Rolling around in the palm of my hand,
Wondering when it will stop rolling.

My mum thinking,
Will it ever be mine again?

It glistens like
The morning dew on the grass.

My mum's ring,
I hope I'll have one like that
When I am older.

Rebecca Whyte (11)
Bushvalley Primary School, Stranocum

My Mum's Lipstick

Bright red,
Like a juicy tomato,
Smooth and slippery
Like a snake's skin.
I rolled it along a wall
Quicker than a lion
Chasing after a dismayed deer.
It smelt like a forest
Of fresh cherries,
While I marked the lipstick
All over my chin, knees and nose.
Why don't they make lipstick
In Mum's shade anymore?

Ashleigh Falconer (11)
Bushvalley Primary School, Stranocum

My Grandad's Shed

Like a ruby nestled
In the corner of the yard,
A secret place for
Me to go to alone.

Shining above me
Like the sun,
And as smooth
As my little face.

Inside, as dark
As a dark night.
Losing my way
In that little world,
Looking for
The big door.
My grandad's shed,
The best of all!

Abbie Patton (11)
Bushvalley Primary School, Stranocum

My Daddy's Combine

A golden giant,
Sat in a ripe lemon field,
The engines roaring
Like lions,
Then eating his prey.
We climbed up onto
An elephant's back,
Then sat on the
Shimmering sun.
We opened the window
And the South Pole's wind
Blew in all around us.
My daddy's combine,
The best of all.

Diane Ramsay (11)
Bushvalley Primary School, Stranocum

My Dad's Quad

The bright red machine,
Painted like
An evening sunset.

It sounded like a lion's roar
That I had never
Heard before.

I was little,
It was big,
The seat was massive
For me to sit.

We rode in the morning,
When I woke up.
We rode in the evening
Before I was tucked up.

The quad was fine
And the memory's mine.

Do you have a quad
Just like my dad and I?

Amy Gibson (10)
Bushvalley Primary School, Stranocum

My See-Saw Tree

My see-saw had a branch
That stuck out like a sore thumb.
The leaves spread green patches of light everywhere,
As if it was raining leaves.
The bark was as wrinkly as a shrivelling plum.
It was as tall as the enormous Eiffel Tower.
I bounced up and down like a jack-in-the-box,
I went so high I touched the sky.
To my surprise I heard a squeak,
Then I fell flat on my face and my cheek.
Why don't trees grow that way anymore?

Clare McGurk (11)
Bushvalley Primary School, Stranocum

The Lane

It's as peaceful as a book,
Echoes like an empty school corridor.
It's as beautiful as a sunny summer's day.
On a snowy winter's day it's like
A curvy, snow-white snake,
Trees are like giants.
From the top of the hill
Houses look like toy cars
In long lines.
The horses gallop in front of trees,
Jumping over logs or fallen branches.
The birds sing short, beautiful songs,
Some romantic, some sweet.
A cow as nosy as a spy,
Chasing you to the top of the hill,
Where you smell the fresh soil.
Light brown, wild rabbits
Scamper through the trees and fields,
Hiding among the long, lush grass.

Mary Patton (11)
Bushvalley Primary School, Stranocum

My Dad's Cowboy Hat

Its colour was black as the darkest night,
Soft to the touch, with a wide rim.
I tried it on, it fell over my eyes,
I dreamt I was a cowgirl living in the Wild West,
I was having so much fun until I fell . . .

As my dad's cowboy hat fell off my head,
I saw the golden buckle,
It shone in the sun
Like a glittering diamond.

As I grew older, the hat disappeared,
Never to be found.
I can't believe they're not in fashion anymore.

Rebecca Wilkinson (10)
Bushvalley Primary School, Stranocum

Recipe For Winter

Take some deep white snow,
Some tasty turkey cooking slowly
And some heavy rain falling down.

Add some red holly berries,
Some playful penguins swimming swiftly
And some freezing snowballs used in snowball fights.

Mix with days of silver frost,
Some cold, slippery ice
And bare trees swaying lightly in the chilly wind.

Decorate with sparkly tinsel dangling down,
Some coloured balls going on the tree
And some cheerful children playing gracefully.

Leave in the freezer
For three long months
And you have made . . . *winter!*

Lauren Bacon (9)
Carnalridge Primary School, Portrush

Recipe For Winter

Take some deep white snow, nice and soft,
Then take some shining icicles hanging from the roof
And then add some nice red juicy berries.

Add some red holly berries
And then add bare trees swaying gently in the wind,
And then get some nice snowdrops growing sweetly.

Mix with days of silver frost,
Some icy wind blowing strongly
And then get a warm fire blazing brightly.

Decorate with a jolly Santa, laughing merrily,
And a big snowman melting slowly.

Leave in the freezer for three long months
And you have made . . . *winter!*

Angus Kelly (9)
Carnalridge Primary School, Portrush

Recipe For Winter!

Take some deep white snow,
Some slippery white ice,
And two singing red robins.

Add some red holly berries,
Some juicy turkey
And a teaspoon of cold wind.

Mix with days of silver frost,
Some magical flying Santas
And a dozen fat snowmen.

Decorate with six long icicles,
Some red, sparkling tinsel
And a pinch of twinkling stars.

Leave in the freezer
For three long months
And you have made . . . *winter!*

Chloe Edgar (9)
Carnalridge Primary School, Portrush

Recipe For Winter

Take some deep white snow,
Some dripping snowflakes falling fast
And shining footprints in the dark.

Add some red holly berries,
Some tasty chilli peppers
And chocolate sprinkles.

Decorate with sparkly tinsel,
Some fairy lights
And sticky toffee.

Leave in the freezer
For three long months
And you have made . . . *winter!*

Lauren Osbourne (9)
Carnalridge Primary School, Portrush

Recipe For Winter

Take some deep white snow,
Some tender turkey
And delicious chicken soup.

Add some steaming hot Christmas pudding,
Some yummy mince pies
And freezing cold ice cream.

Mix with days of silver frost,
Some lovely chocolate fudge cake
And sparkling wine.

Decorate with chocolate sprinkles,
Some icing sugar
And some red holly berries.

Leave in the freezer
For three long months
And you have made . . . *winter!*

Conor McLean (9)
Carnalridge Primary School, Portrush

Recipe For Winter

Take some deep white snow,
Some tasty turkey with hot roast potatoes
And some freezing icicles.

Add some red holly berries,
Some delicious soup, crunchy bread rolls
And cold wine.

Mix with days of silver frost,
Some dangerous snowfalls falling fast,
And sharp snowflakes blowing wildly.

Decorate with Christmas cake,
Some Christmas cards that you make
And sprinkle over some mistletoe.

Leave in the freezer
For three long months
And you have made . . . *winter!*

Robert Simpson (9)
Carnalridge Primary School, Portrush

Recipe For Winter

Take some deep white snow,
Some nice warm turkey
And some icy snowflakes.

Add some red holly berries,
Some really icy roads
And some tremendous snowmen.

Mix with days of silver frost,
Some strong, windy gales,
And some sparkling icicles.

Decorate with some big Christmas baubles,
Some small children playing
And some big Christmas trees.

Leave in the freezer
For three long months
And you have made . . . *winter!*

Matthew McLaughlin (9)
Carnalridge Primary School, Portrush

Recipe For Winter

Take some deep white snow,
Some Christmas pudding
And icy roads.

Add some red holly berries,
Some frozen rivers
And snowmen.

Mix with some days of silver frost,
Some snowflakes
And tinsel.

Decorate with some ivy,
Some tree beads
And some ice skating.

Leave in the freezer
For three long months
And you have made . . . *winter!*

Andrew Holmes (9)
Carnalridge Primary School, Portrush

Recipe For Winter

Take some deep white snow,
Some little stars shining brightly,
And cold wind howling ferociously.

Add some red holly berries,
Some juicy turkey
And red robins singing sweetly.

Mix with days of silver frost,
A magical flying Santa
And a dozen fat snowmen.

Decorate with long icicles,
Some sparkling silver tinsel
And some excited children playing happily.

Leave in the freezer
For three long months
And you have made . . . *winter!*

Shannon Peters (9)
Carnalridge Primary School, Portrush

Recipe For Winter

Take some deep white snow,
Some tasty turkey cooking slowly
And some heavy rain.

Add some red holly berries,
Some lovely snowflakes falling down
And some slippery ice melting quickly.

Mix with days of silver frost,
Some children singing merrily
And some icicles dripping down.

Decorate with some coloured bulbs,
Some lovely tinsel, sparkling beautifully
And some golden stars shining brightly.

Leave in the freezer
For three months
And you have made . . . *winter!*

Anna Dallas (8)
Carnalridge Primary School, Portrush

Recipe For Winter

Take some deep white snow,
Some icicles, long and spindly,
Hanging from the rooftops,
And some bitterly cold wind
Gusting wildly to the east.

Add some red holly berries,
Some bare branches blowing up and down
Almost touching the ground,
And don't forget Mr Robin Redbreast's sweet little tune.

Mix with days of silver frost,
Some pale people in the town,
Hurrying, scurrying in the snow,
And penguins waddling here and there
In the Antarctic, scurrying everywhere.

Decorate the Christmas tree just before lunch,
Some shiny tinsel on the tree
And bobbles hanging from every branch.
How many are there?
One, two and three.

Leave in the freezer
For three long months
And you have made . . . *winter!*

Amber Macfarlane (8)
Carnalridge Primary School, Portrush

Winter Ingredients

Take some deep white snow,
Some tasty brown turkey from the oven
And lots of cold snowflakes drifting down.

Add some red holly berries,
Some red robins singing sweetly
And some icy icicles falling fast.

Mix with days of silver frost,
Some joyful Christmas spirit
And a happy Santa Claus with his elves.

Decorate with some nice Christmas presents,
Some joyful Christmas cards,
Some wet, hard hailstones.

Leave it in the freezer
For three long months
And you have made . . . *winter!*

When you have made winter,
Try to make summer because
It's freezing out here!

Glen Campbell (9)
Carnalridge Primary School, Portrush

Recipe For Winter

Take some deep white snow,
Some brown tasty turkey,
And some lovely red robins singing sweetly.

Add some red holly berries,
Some white sparkly snowflakes,
And some ice-cold icicles dangling spindly.

Mix with days of silver frost,
Some happy cheerful children playing,
And a jolly Santa delivering toys.

Decorate with,
Some bright twinkly stars shining down
And a beautiful colourful Christmas tree.

Leave in the freezer for
Three long months,
And now you have made . . .
Winter!

Victoria Logan (9)
Carnalridge Primary School, Portrush

A Winter Recipe

Take some deep white snow,
Some delicious mince pies, steaming hot,
And a few sharp, glittery icicles
Clinging tightly to the eaves.

Add some red holly berries,
Some fruity sweets sitting in the sweetie box,
And one bar of Galaxy chocolate,
Melting deliciously on the counter.

Mix with days of silver frost,
Some ice from a frozen pond, sparkling beautifully,
And some white snow falling gracefully and gently.

Decorate with silver, tinkling bells,
Some colourful lights twinkling brightly
And squeeze on some sparkly white icing.

Leave in the freezer
For three long months
And you have made . . . *winter!*

Caitlin Buick (8)
Carnalridge Primary School, Portrush

Recipe For Winter

Take some deep white snow,
Some white snowflakes falling
And some icicles dripping down.

Add some red holly berries,
Some red robins singing loudly
And some bitterly cold wind
Gusting wildly to the east.

Mix with a day of silver frost,
Some reindeer flying swiftly,
And Rudolph guiding the herd
With his bright red shiny nose.

Decorate with snowmen melting slowly,
Some silver tinsel placed proudly
And children skating quickly.

Leave in the freezer
For three long months
And you have made . . . *winter!*

Eva McBride (8)
Carnalridge Primary School, Portrush

Ingredients For Winter

Take some deep white snow,
Some cold ice
And icicles.

Add some red holly berries,
Some blue fairy lights
And snowflakes.

Mix with days of silver frost,
Some freezing icicles
And some sparkly snow.

Decorate with some tinsel,
Some tree lights
And some Christmas tree balls.

Leave in the freezer
For three long months
And you have made . . . *winter!*

Chelsea Greer   (9)
Carnalridge Primary School, Portrush

Ingredients For Winter

Take some deep white snow,
Some freezing ice
And some icicles.

Add some red holly berries,
Some blue fairy lights
And snowflakes falling gracefully.

Mix with days of silver frost,
Some freezing icicles hanging from rooftops
And some sparkly snow falling slowly from the cold sky.

Decorate with some shining tinsel,
Some Christmas tree lights that shine through the window
And some Christmas tree balls and a star on top.

Leave in the freezer
For three long months
And you have made . . . *winter!*

Shannon-Lee Mitchell (9)
Carnalridge Primary School, Portrush

Recipe For Winter

Take some deep white snow,
Some white, sparkling tinsel draping beautifully,
And some strong, wild wind that could blow you off your feet.

Add some red holly berries,
Some blue flashing fairy lights
And icy cold snowflakes falling like stars.

Mix with days of silver frost,
Some busy, working elves
And some happy, laughing children.

Decorate with long icicles,
Some hot, plump Christmas pudding
And a pinch of twinkling stars shimmering brightly.

Leave in the freezer
For three long months
And you have made . . . *winter!*

Sarah Medcalf (8)
Carnalridge Primary School, Portrush

Recipe For Winter

Take some deep white snow,
Some icy cold hailstones
And stir with bright gold snowflakes.

Add some red holly berries,
Some green Christmas tree leaves
And stir with some sparkly tinsel.

Mix with days of silver frost,
Some gleaming icicles hanging from the roofs
And add some baubles from the tree.

Decorate with green, prickly holly leaves,
Some flashing blue lights from the tree
And put in a lovely green Christmas tree.

Now leave in the freezer
For three long months
And you have made . . . *winter!*

Kirsty Rebecca Millar (8)
Carnalridge Primary School, Portrush

Recipe For Winter

Take some deep white snow,
Some cold ice and mucky grass
And a tiny red robin singing sweetly.

Add some red holly berries,
Some juicy, tasty turkey
Surrounded by vegetables
And covered in gravy.

Mix with days of silver frost,
Some crisp green grass
And bare trees.

Decorate with shining stars at night,
Some children sledging and having fun.

Leave in the freezer
For three long months
And you have made . . . *winter!*

Robert Downs (9)
Carnalridge Primary School, Portrush

Recipe For Winter

Take some deep white snow,
Some white sparkling snowflakes
And some long, sharp, twisting icicles.

Add some nice red holly berries,
Some soft white snow
And some gold, sparkling tinsel.

Mix with days of silver frost,
Some big white snowmen
And some slippery white snow.

Decorate with a jolly Santa,
Some very excited children
And decorated Christmas trees.

Leave in the freezer
For three long months
And you have made . . . *winter!*

Peter Minihan (8)
Carnalridge Primary School, Portrush

Recipe For Winter

Take some deep white snow,
Some sparkling icicles
And snowflakes.
Add some red holly berries,
Some tasty turkey
And lovely ham.
Mix with days of silver frost,
Some lovely new toys from old Santa
And the hard wind blowing.
Decorate with mistletoe,
Some holly
And a scarf.
Leave in the freezer
For three long months
And you have made . . . *winter!*

Matthew Leighton (9)
Carnalridge Primary School, Portrush

Love

Love is red like hearts.
Love smells like fresh rose petals.
Love tastes like runny chocolate.
Love sounds like ringing bells on a wedding day
In church on a sunny day.
Love looks like two people kissing.
Love feels like soft, furry, heart-shaped red cushions.
Love reminds me of big red lips!
Love, love, love!

Zara Loughridge (11)
Carrowreagh Primary School, Ballymoney

Happiness

Happiness is yellow like vanilla ice cream.
It sounds like M&D's.
It tastes like ice lollies.
It smells like ice cream.
It looks like M&D's.
It feels like ice lollies.
It reminds me of holidays.

Ryan Moon (10)
Carrowreagh Primary School, Ballymoney

Anger

Anger is red like fire.
It feels like your blood is boiling.
It reminds me of a raging bull.
Anger looks like a hurricane.
Anger smells like spilt blood.
Anger tastes like strawberries and cream.
Anger sounds like a raging bull.

David McAneaney (11)
Carrowreagh Primary School, Ballymoney

Happiness

Happiness is yellow.
Happiness is yellow like daffodils.
Happiness smells like strawberries and cream.
It tastes like milk chocolate eggs,
It sounds like birds tweeting in the trees,
It looks like fresh flowers,
It feels like swimming in the sea,
It reminds me of summer holidays.

Shannon Steele (10)
Carrowreagh Primary School, Ballymoney

Summer

The summertime is coming
And the trees are sweetly blooming,
Everything beautiful in sight
And everywhere children are playing in the street.
The laughter I hear so sweet.
Everybody is having a barbecue,
My mum is having one too.
The smell of sausages roasting over the barbecue,
That lovely smell of hot dogs.
I wake up and it was just a dream.
That's what makes it so special . . .

Demi Clarke (10)
Currie Primary School, Belfast

Working Dogs

There are many working dogs
And we appreciate them.
And if you don't believe me
You'd better read this poem then.

St Bernards help lost people in the snow.
Alsatians guard our property.
Labradors show blind people where to go.
Border collies round up sheep.

Huskies pull sleighs through the ice.
Don't you think that's really nice?

There are many working dogs
And we appreciate them.
Now you'd better believe me
Or you've not read this poem yet.

Leah Ruddock (9)
Doagh Primary School, Doagh

Why? Why? Why?

Sometimes I lie in my bed
And think of what my dad has said.

Why snow is so white
And why I go to bed at night?

And why water is so blue
And why I have got red shoes?

I think to myself, *is this all true?*
Of all the things I see and do.

Stacey Mackay (8)
Doagh Primary School, Doagh

Portrush

Portrush smells of the salty sea,
Fish and chips and popcorn and candy.

Portrush sounds like noisy amusements, the sea,
seagulls screeching,
Screaming children and the motorbikes at the North West.

Portrush looks like busy shops full of people,
Rows of caravans, the Big Dipper and Ramore Head.

Portrush feels like the sun in your face, sand between your toes,
The spray of the sea and wasps stinging you.

Portrush tastes like ice cream, meaty burgers, battered fish,
Melted chocolate, greasy chips, the salty sea and fizzy lemonade.

Jack Francey (9)
Doagh Primary School, Doagh

What's The Weather?

Is it sun?
Is it snow?
Is it rain?
We just don't know!
What can the weather be
From all the clouds on top of me?
The sun?
The snow?
We just don't know!
Oh look it's rain!
Or is it snow?
I can't tell by the clouds!
I just don't know!

Molly Piper (8)
Doagh Primary School, Doagh

Rugby

I go to rugby on a Saturday,
All kitted out to play.
Come rain or hail or shine
We're there at nine in a line.

Our training starts and off we run,
The coaches like to have some fun.
Press-ups, tackles, running for miles,
Draining our energy, the coaches all smile.

At matches we all run around,
To the sound
Of our parents shouting instructions,
Which are bound to cause ructions!

Matthew Hamilton (9)
Doagh Primary School, Doagh

Animals

A pig is a very dirty animal.
It rolls in the mud.
But when the pig needs a wash,
All you can see are dirty soap suds!

A cow helps us by giving milk,
But to do this it must eat grass,
Or else it could end up like . . .
An ass!

A chicken is the fox's prey,
I'm sure it prays at night.
But when the foxes come,
The chickens have such a fright!

Peter Gordon (8)
Doagh Primary School, Doagh

My Alien

An alien came into my garden
He was awfully big and green
He had one eye on his forehead
And I thought I was going to scream.

He told me he'd come from outer space
And that his name was Jack
He said he had come such a long way
And he didn't want to go back.

So I let him stay in my garden
'Thank you Simon,' he said
He doesn't have to go back to his planet
Because now he lives in my shed!

Simon Bell (9)
Doagh Primary School, Doagh

Holidays

Holidays are brilliant fun
And in the summer you can get some sun
But when there is rain
There is nothing to gain
From being in a different country.

Holidays are a chance to visit old landmarks
And to visit historic ships like the Cutty Sark
You can even take a ride on a D-Day landing craft
And hope it doesn't become a submarine!

Christopher Graham (10)
Doagh Primary School, Doagh

Ashley Tisdale

Ashley Tisdale is so cool
I wish I could hang out with her
Why don't we go to the pool?
If only I could meet her.

Ashley has two dogs called Blondie and Shadow
I like them very much
I've got a picture of her on my window
High up where no one can touch.

I'm Ashley's biggest fan
She can act, sing and dance
I always write about her
The boys all love her too, she leaves them in a trance.

Amy Sands (8)
Doagh Primary School, Doagh

Baby Sam

At my childminder's
There is this little baby boy,
He's one year old.
I kiss and hold him tight
For this little man had to fight for his life.

I really should tell you that
This little man was 10 weeks early.
But now he's strong,
He eats all he can for this little man is baby *Sam!*

Hannah Magee (10)
Doagh Primary School, Doagh

Weather, Weather

The sun is bright,
The sun is bright,
It shines on me.
I like it very much
Because it brightens up
The summer days.

Drip, drip, drip
Goes the rain.
It splatters on me and you.
So when the rain splatters on me
I go back to my cosy home.

Bang! Crash!
Goes the thunder.
Crash! Bang!
Goes the lightning.
But the poor animals hate that sound
Very, very much.

So weather, weather
Out of those three,
I think the sun
Would be the right one for me.

Ben White (9)
Doagh Primary School, Doagh

Bear

I had a bear
I lost him in the park
When I found him
I put him in my heart.

I took him home and bathed him
And gave him lots of love
I'm so glad my bear is with me
To give me back that love.

Megan Robinson (9)
Doagh Primary School, Doagh

Grandad

I loved to walk with my grandad,
I saw him every day,
When we walked he never said hurry up.

We always made stuff out of wood,
Trains, planes, boats
And fishing rods and we laughed
At all the good times.

We always told ghost stories,
He always made the most frightening ones.
One day there was thunder and lightning,
We went out and watched it,
In the happy days.

I walked with him every day
And I loved him to go fishing with me,
But that will never happen again.
But now I am happy
That he is in a better place.

Stafford Lynn (10)
Doagh Primary School, Doagh

The Jockey

The jockey is crimson red and midnight-black
She is summer
In the jumping arena
She is sunny.
A jockey is a red and black riding jacket
A smart, polished riding crop
She is 'National Velvet'
A crisp, green apple.

Georgia Stocker (10)
Greenisland Primary School, Greenisland

Sir Patrick Moore

Sir Patrick Moore is a dark black
He is all seasons
In an observatory and a TV studio
He is very cloudy
Sir Patrick Moore is a monocle
A high-powered telescope
He is 'The Sky at Night'
He is mushy peas.

Peter Bothwell (11)
Greenisland Primary School, Greenisland

Wizard

A wizard is purple,
He is autumn,
In a dark, gloomy castle.
He is cold and dark midnight,
A wizard in a large cloak,
A long crooked wand,
He is Harry Potter,
A dead toad.

Aaron Gorman (11)
Greenisland Primary School, Greenisland

SAS Soldier

An SAS soldier is in green camo'
He is hidden in summer in a training camp
He is wet weather
An SAS soldier wears a camo' helmet
An M4 carbine assault rifle
He is 'Ultimate Force'
A tin of beans.

Scott Beattie (10)
Greenisland Primary School, Greenisland

The Builder

A builder is yellow, blue, white and black,
He is the summer,
He works everywhere,
He is a bright, sunny day,
A builder is yellow or white hard hat,
A nail gun,
He is 'Bob the Builder',
A jar of pickles.

Wesley Strange (11)
Greenisland Primary School, Greenisland

The Farmer

A farmer is blue, red and white.
He is sunny spring.
In a farm he is warm and sunny.
A farmer is a big, straw hat.
A big combine harvester.
He is 'Kill it, Cook it, Eat it!'
A full farmhouse fry up.

Stephen Quinn (11)
Greenisland Primary School, Greenisland

Soldier

A soldier is green
He is summer
In barracks
He is like thunder
A soldier wears body armour
A SMG AK47 machine gun
He is in 'Ross Kemp in Afghanistan'
A bowl of vegetable soup.

Jordan Pollock (11)
Greenisland Primary School, Greenisland

Ventriloquist

A ventriloquist is black
He is autumn
In a shopping centre he is mild
A ventriloquist wears a tuxedo
A wooden dummy
He is 'Sooty and Sweep'
A piece of fruit.

Carter McIlwain (11)
Greenisland Primary School, Greenisland

Assassin

An assassin wears dark black.
He is winter.
In a meeting place or headquarters
He is like rain.
A dark black colour, leather legs.
A sleeping drug or a poison drug.
He is in the 'Assassins' Creed'.
A mayo and chicken sandwich.

Lee McAlister (10)
Greenisland Primary School, Greenisland

Footballer

A footballer is red and white
He is three seasons
In a big stadium
He is all round weather
A footballer is shirts, shorts and long socks
A Nike football
He is 'Match of the Day'
An energy drink.

Jeremy Martin (11)
Greenisland Primary School, Greenisland

The Swimming Teacher

A swimming teacher is turquoise-blue,
She is summer,
In a swimming centre
She is a raining storm,
A swimming teacher is flip-flops,
A silver, shiny whistle,
'The Olympics',
A ham and lettuce sandwich.

Lesley Greer (11)
Greenisland Primary School, Greenisland

Tiger Woods

Tiger Woods is bright red and black
He is the summer
On the green golf course
He is sunny
Tiger Woods is Nike all over
A silver golf club
He is 'PGA Tour'
A big bowl of salad.

James Rice (11)
Greenisland Primary School, Greenisland

A Footballer

A footballer, a red, white and black,
She is summertime,
In Anfield on a football pitch,
She is a flower on a sunny day.
A footballer is a sweaty pair of shin pads,
A pair of blue striped football boots,
She is 'Bend It Like Beckham',
A juicy red apple.

Emily Harris (11)
Greenisland Primary School, Greenisland

The Builder

A builder is red and blue checked,
He is all seasons,
In any places there is work to be done,
He is a cold, dark winter,
A builder is jeans and a helmet,
A hammer and nails with a ladder,
He is 'Bob the Builder',
A strong cup of tea and an egg sandwich.

Aimee Douglas (10)
Greenisland Primary School, Greenisland

An Irish Dancer

An Irish dancer is blue, black and purple,
She is a bright summer,
In a dance hall,
She is a sunny day.
An Irish dancer is a dancing dress,
A pair of pumps and treble shoes,
She is 'Tina O'Brien',
A bottle of water.

Elana Dickson (10)
Greenisland Primary School, Greenisland

Cricketer

Freddie Flintoff is white
He is three seasons
In the Oval ground
He is a sunny day
Freddie is a bat, helmet and pads
A round red ball
He is 'The Ashes'
A Lucozade Sport energy drink.

Ryan Duddy (11)
Greenisland Primary School, Greenisland

An Ice Hockey Player

An ice hockey player is a dark red and blue
He is winter
In an ice rink
He is icy weather
An ice hockey player wears a top, trousers and shorts
An ice hockey stick and a helmet
He is AHL on FSPA
An orange.

Peter Noble (10)
Greenisland Primary School, Greenisland

A Teacher

A teacher is a pair of trousers and a stripy tie
He is summer
In a school building
He is snow
A teacher is a checked shirt
A workshop full of machines
He is 'Waterloo Road'
A bacon, lettuce and tomato baguette.

Emma Curtis (11)
Greenisland Primary School, Greenisland

Mr Blair

Our teacher is light blue
He is summer
He works in the best school ever
He is the glorious sun
Our teacher is a dark blue striped tie
A Mercedes that's hot red
'The Teacher Show'
A big red apple.

Naomi Bradshaw (11)
Greenisland Primary School, Greenisland

Wind

When the wind blows
Your hat will blow off.

When the wind blows
Trees can fall down.

When the wind blows
The waves will splash.

When the wind blows
Windmills will turn.

When the wind blows
Doors will crash shut.

When the wind blows
Kites will fly high.

When the wind blows
Dustbins will flap up and down.

When the wind blows
Umbrellas will turn inside out.

Stephen Fee (10)
Greenisland Primary School, Greenisland

Wind

It blows slates off roofs,
It rushes down chimneys,
It roars like a lion,
And sounds like a fire.

Window frames creak
And waves start to break.
Doors slam shut,
The wind is awake.

Flags start to flutter
And paper scatters,
Bin lids clatter
And a tree crashes.

David McClements (9)
Greenisland Primary School, Greenisland

Wind

The wind is a monster
Winning a battle.
It scares little children
And makes things rattle.

It messes up your hair
And bangs at doors.
It sounds like a bear
And bounces off shores.

It makes scarves flutter
And brings down trees.
It dances around windows
And rattles your knees.

It crashes into flowers
And chases leaves.
But then it all stops
And it's just a breeze.

Samuel Brolly (10)
Greenisland Primary School, Greenisland

Wind

It pulls at umbrellas,
It howls down chimneys,
It makes people cold
And shivers all day.

It crashes at windows
And blows down trees.
It makes leaves dance
And branches shake.

It sounds like whispers
Of people talking.
It makes scarves blow
And dogs bark.

Emily Robinson (9)
Greenisland Primary School, Greenisland

Wind

Wind can be irritating,
It pulls up your skirt,
It messes with your hair
And turns your umbrella inside out.

Leaves off the trees flutter,
Cans on the road roll down the hill,
Trees fall down,
Washing lines could break.

Signposts breaks,
Bins will tip,
Branches fall on the roads,
Waves come flying up.

Darcy Osborne (10)
Greenisland Primary School, Greenisland

Wind

It races through my clothes,
It runs through my hair,
It chases dogs
To make people scared.

It crashes into dustbins,
It creeps into houses,
It rattles at the window,
It slams the door.

It breaks down trees,
It scatters leaves,
It rushes past skyscrapers,
Now it's after me!

Stephanie Beck (10)
Greenisland Primary School, Greenisland

Wind

I wake up in the morning,
I walk outside,
The wind is blowing in my eyes,
I can hear waves collide.

I go to the washing,
I hear it flap
And then it blows away my hat.
All I can hear is the wind's tap.

I drop my book,
So I bend on down,
The wind then blows all around,
But I'm inside now safe and sound.

I can hear the wind shaking, stirring,
Wild things are occurring,
My door swings open, now I am scared.
I cannot describe the things I have heard.

Rachel Hall (9)
Greenisland Primary School, Greenisland

Wind

It is here once again,
Up to its tricks again.
It is back once again,
The monster is back.

It blows stuff away
And breaks stuff again.
It makes noises like a lion
And scares you at night.

Hats blow off, leaves fly off trees,
Doors slam and kites fly away,
By one thing only
And that's wind.

Alison Loney (9)
Greenisland Primary School, Greenisland

Wind

It howls when it's angry,
When it's excited it swirls.
When it's calm it whispers,
When it's happy it twirls.

It comes up behind you,
It gives you a scare,
But it seems to me
The wind doesn't care.

It rustles the leaves,
It makes the rubbish scatter,
It blows down the trees,
It makes dustbin lids clatter.

It powers windmills,
In the wind I can fly a kite.
It rustles at day
And it howls at night.

Niamh Carroll (10)
Greenisland Primary School, Greenisland

Wind

The wind is a breeze,
It makes such a clatter,
It flaps past flags,
It makes our teeth chatter.

The wind is a chase,
It sneaks past the trees,
It flies around our chimneys,
It rushes through the seas.

The wind is a whistle,
It makes a loud sound,
It scatters among the leaves
And bangs down on the ground.

Jennifer Rice (9)
Greenisland Primary School, Greenisland

Wind

It blows off your hat,
It spins the leaves round,
It stirs up the waves
And pulls the trees down.

It whistles and howls,
It flies with the birds,
It flaps and flutters
All the flags that it sees.

It slams all the doors,
It crawls through gaps,
It captures kites
And lets them fly free.

It flips umbrellas
And turns them around.
It teases little children
And rattles their windows.

Peter Macartney (9)
Greenisland Primary School, Greenisland

Wind

When the wind blows
Things are always happening.

When the wind blows
It always goes rudely past unlike its little sister Breeze.

When the wind blows
It always fears big brother Hurricane.

John Griffiths (9)
Greenisland Primary School, Greenisland

Wind

When the wind blows
It sounds like a whistle.

When the wind blows
It blows down bins.

When the wind blows
It makes a loud clatter.

When the wind blows
It makes paper scatter.

When the wind blows
It blows plastic bags.

When the wind blows
It makes you lose your balance.

When the wind blows
It takes your breath away.

Corey Clarke (9)
Greenisland Primary School, Greenisland

Wind

It's like a howling sound,
Wind makes you feel miserable,
It blows different things down streets,
Pulls at your clothes.

It blows at your hat,
Flags flutter, leaves mutter,
Tree blow down,
Makes you feel worn out.

Sounds like wolves howling,
Doors slam,
Windows clatter,
Wind is the matter.

Judithe Allen (10)
Greenisland Primary School, Greenisland

Wind

It makes dustbins clatter
Leaves flutter
But when my umbrella blows inside out
It does matter.

It scares the dogs
Windmills turn
Kites rush
It rolls the logs.

It makes skyscrapers unsteady
The branches on the trees groan
The flowers will all die
My screams are ready.

Jodie McCann (10)
Greenisland Primary School, Greenisland

Wind

It blows off your hat,
It whistles like a drier.
It scares your cat
But it never will tire.

It shatters your windows
And blows up your clothes.
It can destroy your shows
And freezes off your toes.

Your doors will slam,
It flutters like a flag
And breaks up a dam
And it's always such a drag.

Jason Fleming (10)
Greenisland Primary School, Greenisland

Wind

It crashes on skyscrapers
It dances on waves
It hides in dustbins
And it breaks the silence.

It rustles with leaves
It cheers on flowers
It will chase the sloe
It squeezes through windows.

It roars when angry
And whistles when calm
It's hard to breathe
And it fights with branches.

It smashes against the walls
It chases anything in sight
It's slow in a breeze
And fast in a gale.

It's cold on your face
And freezes dogs
It's annoying in your house
And runs into windmills.

Steven Hart (10)
Greenisland Primary School, Greenisland

Wind

When the wind blows
Waves crash, wolves howl.

When the wind blows
Umbrellas fly, doors slam.

When the wind blows
Dustbins flap, windows creak.

When the wind blows
Dogs bark and skirts blow up.

Charlotte Lavery (9)
Greenisland Primary School, Greenisland

Happiness

Happiness is when I visit a funfair.
I'm excited when I'm on my favourite ride.
Happiness is when I'm playing my PSP
Enjoying my favourite game.
Happiness is when I'm in the park or at the beach
Playing with my friends.
Happiness is Christmas morning
When I open my presents.
Happiness is when your favourite football team wins a match.
Happiness is when you go to the cinema to see a movie.
Happiness is when you get a DVD or game that you wanted.

Philip Martin (10)
Greystone Primary School, Antrim

Darkness Is . . .

Darkness is when you are in the dark woods.
Darkness is when you fall unconscious.
Darkness is when you are in your bedroom at night.
Darkness is when you are buried alive.
Darkness is when you are in the cinema alone.
Darkness is when your friend is hurt badly and is taken to hospital.
Darkness is when you are stuck in a tunnel with a vicious dog.

Blair Neeson (11)
Greystone Primary School, Antrim

Bob The Whale

There once was a whale named Bob
Who looked like an enormous blob.
He liked eating fish
Served up on a dish,
He also liked corn on the cob.

Lois Lafferty (11)
Greystone Primary School, Antrim

Excitement Is . . .

Excitement is when your favourite football team scores a goal.
Excitement happens when you can't wait for something special
to happen.
Excitement is when you go to watch a football match.

Excitement happens when you can't wait until Christmas.
Excitement is when you have no patience to go on holiday.
Excitement is when you are about to get your driver's licence.

Excitement happens when you win something very special.
Excitement is when you go on a trip with your friends.
Excitement is when you can't wait for your birthday.

Jordan Sloan (11)
Greystone Primary School, Antrim

A Young Girl

There was a young girl who played hockey
Who would much rather have been a jockey
She went to look at a pony
But they were all far too bony
So she decided to stick with the hockey.

Rebecca Elizabeth Kennedy (11)
McKinney Primary School, Dundrod

Trumpet

T his musical instrument
R umbles sometimes
U nder your nose
M ostly on your mouth
P laying away
E xactly as you want it
T his musical instrument.

Caleb McNaul (11)
McKinney Primary School, Dundrod

Spring

S unshine, light showers and breeze,
P oppies, snowdrops and sweet peas,
R ustling trees,
I n the hedges there are buzzing bees,
N esting birds in the trees,
G lorious springtime.

Jane Hannah Susan Kirkpatrick (11)
McKinney Primary School, Dundrod

Spring

S un sitting up in the sky
P eople are picking flowers
R abbits bouncing up and down
I ntelligent foxes finding their food
N oisy animals messing around
G rass growing everywhere.

Sophie Clarke (11)
McKinney Primary School, Dundrod

Lambs

L ook at them pounce about
A lways so happy
M others always busy
B undles of fun
S een in spring.

Kaitlyn Hannah McKeown (11)
McKinney Primary School, Dundrod

Riddle

Riddle me this, riddle me that,
Guess my riddle or perhaps not
I whisper in the wind
I have one leg
I shave my hair in winter
I grow it in the summer.

What am I?
A: A tree.

David John Graham (11)
McKinney Primary School, Dundrod

Mountains

A bump in the ground,
They're sure and sound.

A rolling hillside
Where animals hide.

Eagle shadows wipe the floor
While up above high peaks they soar.

The mountains are still standing here
After many a year, a year, a year . . .

Hannah Johnston (10)
McKinney Primary School, Dundrod

Pig - Cinquain

Piggy
Pink and smelly
Grunting, eating, sleeping
All alone in their muddy sty
Porker.

Kate Taggart (11)
McKinney Primary School, Dundrod

The Salmon Run

Heading back to the place I was born,
the only place where I can spawn.

It's good to leave the sea behind,
my birthplace I have to find.

Many dangers lie ahead
before I reach my spawning bed.

So many predators around every bend,
it makes you feel like you haven't got a friend.

Even when I'm exhausted I continue to climb waterfalls,
I cannot be distracted, I must follow nature's call.

I've managed it, I'm here,
I'll eat a little fly or some other tasty morsel and breed before I die.

Kori Quinn Leckey (10)
McKinney Primary School, Dundrod

Lorries - Cinquain

Lorry
Pulling machine
Fuel tanker, grain trailer
Comes in all sizes big and small
Lorries.

Jamie Anderson (11)
McKinney Primary School, Dundrod

Charolais - Haiku

Fat, white and quiet
Dreaming of eating silage
Beautiful cattle.

Christopher Collier (10)
McKinney Primary School, Dundrod

Colour Poem

Red is for the fire that the Devil's house is made of.
Red is the fury that we all have.

Orange is the colour of pumpkins at Hallowe'en.
Orange is the sunset which is in the afternoon.
Orange is for leaves which fall off the trees.

Yellow is the colour of the sun.
Yellow is happy, how we all feel.
Yellow makes me feel enthusiastic about the things I do.

Green is for the growing green grass.
Green is nature which makes me feel alive.
Green is Ireland which is different shades of green.

Blue is the colour of the diamond-blue sea.
Blue is the colour of aquamarine.
Blue makes me feel relaxed.

Purple is royalty which the king and the queen have.
Purple is the veins which go through your body.
Purple is the blueberries which we pick in summer.

Reece Black (8)
Parkgate Primary School, Parkgate

Colour Poem

Red is the colour of red rubies.
Orange is the colour of the sunset.
Yellow is the colour of the warm sunshine.
Green is the colour of the soft green grass.
Blue is the colour of us when we are cold.
Purple is the colour of the soft blueberries.

James McFarland (8)
Parkgate Primary School, Parkgate

Colour Poem

Red is the scarlet cherries we eat.
Red is the crimson leaves that fall at autumn.

Orange is the happy people who go outside to play.
Orange is the sunset which shines in the sky.

Bronze is the cheerful faces at Christmas.
Yellow is the sun which makes the sky bright.

Green is the lime tortoise which moves.
Green is the nature we see around the world.

Blue is the calm sea which waves.
Blue is the peaceful sky.

Purple is the veins that run down their hand.
Purple is the soft blueberries in a pie.

Thomas McAdoo (8)
Parkgate Primary School, Parkgate

Colour Poem

Red is the fire that burns away,
Red is the night, the shepherd's delight.

Orange is the fruit we all like to eat,
Oranges, peaches, apricots and more are all full of vitamin C.

Yellow is bright, fun and happy,
Yellow lemons are very, very sour.

Green is for lime, we sometimes put in Coke,
Green is for moss all over the ground.

Blue is for topaz that sparkles and glows,
Blue is for navy, all soft and woolly.

Purple is for violet, sometimes used in poems,
Purple is for lilac, a very light purple.

Jordan Barron (9)
Parkgate Primary School, Parkgate

Colour Poem

Red is the colour of my crimson cheeks.
Red is for the colour of my ruby lips.

Blue is for my sapphire eyes.
Blue is for the topaz sea.

Green is for the trees that sway in the wind.
Green is for a tortoise shell.

A yellow, amber and apricot sunset.
A yellow and bronze flower that makes my day.

Amethyst is the gemstone that sparkles all night.
Blueberry muffins all warm and juicy, yummy!

Amber is the colour of the traffic lights
And American sunsets at night.

Thomas Sherry (9)
Parkgate Primary School, Parkgate

Colour Poem

Red is the shepherd's delight,
Red is for the teacher's uniform.

Orange is the colour of vitamin C,
Orange is the fruit that grows in a tree.

Yellow is the sun in the sky,
That warms our world.

Green is jealousy,
Slippery moss on planks of wood.

Blue is the sea in the morning light,
Feeling cold in the night.

Purple tulips dancing in the wind,
Blood running through our veins.

Morgan Chambers (9)
Parkgate Primary School, Parkgate

Colour Poem

Red is for Man U,
They call themselves the Red Devils.

Orange like the sunset,
Vitamin C too.

Yellow, warm and cheerful like the sun,
Inspiration and courage like bronze or gold.

Green, emerald, jade and moss means Ireland rules,
Green means jealousy and envy.

Blue is the colour of the sky,
Cold, calm and quiet.

Purple is an amethyst,
It is also royalty.

Mark Davidson (8)
Parkgate Primary School, Parkgate

Colour Poem

Red is the fire that burns the house
And is the colour that brings us fury.

Orange is a sunset that will just show
It is the colour that makes us happy.

Yellow is the sun all nice and warm,
The cheerful children laughing and loving.

Green is the emeralds shining and lime,
It is the ivy that brings our friendship alive.

Blue makes us feel blue,
It makes us feel blue.

Purple is the royalty in the crown,
It is our veins that run through our body.

Celine Auld (8)
Parkgate Primary School, Parkgate

Love

The colour of love is lavender.
The smell of love is fragrant roses.
The sound of love is sweet music.
The taste of love is melted chocolates.
Love looks like Heaven.
Love feels as light as a feather.
Love is fabulous.

Robert Ellison (11)
Parkgate Primary School, Parkgate

Panda

The panda is soft and cuddly
With eyes black and shiny like buttons.
It crunches on bamboo high in the mountains.
They are black and white like a sheepdog.
They are the best animal there is.
I think they are the best, do you?

Claire Shannon (9)
Parkgate Primary School, Parkgate

Anger

Anger is purple and red,
It tastes like red-hot chilli peppers,
It looks like decaying flowers turning black,
It sounds like the blast of heavy metal music,
Anger feels like an explosion inside me,
Anger is unhappy.

Lauren Miniss (10)
Parkgate Primary School, Parkgate

The Tiger

Tiger, tiger in the night
You make me shiver and shake with fright.
Your eyes are like a burning fire.
Stalking everything in your path,
Until finally you pounce as fast as lightning
And your prey falls dead in front of your eyes.

Kirsty Simpson (10)
Parkgate Primary School, Parkgate

The Beautiful Cheetah

The cheetah silent, yet heard throughout the animal kingdom.
Lightweight, yet strong and powerful.
Sneaky, yet as fast as the wind.
She combines her forces to do what she does best; hunt.
Her prey cannot do a thing as she patiently waits,
Then she pounces, her jagged claws spring from her paws like a
deadly jack-in-the-box.
Then she brings home food for another night.

Nicole McCammond (11)
Parkgate Primary School, Parkgate

The Dolphin

The dolphin glides through the water
And leaps like an acrobat into the air
Its skin is as smooth as silk.

Farrah Neeson (9)
Parkgate Primary School, Parkgate

Colour Poem

Red is the colour of the rising sun.
Red is embarrassed, blushing and gore.
Red is angry, fiery and hot.

Orange is juicy, bouncy, fun.
Orange is the colour of the setting sun.
Orange is apricots we eat every day.

Yellow is the glory on people's faces.
Yellow is the sunlight that everybody likes.
Yellow is warm and cheerful and makes you smile.

Green is nature that God made for us.
Green is moss on your garden wall.
Green is jealousy that all of us have sometimes.

Blue is cold but makes us calm.
Blue is ice on your garden.
Blue is turquoise, the colour of some cars.

Purple is royalty, kings and queens.
Purple is blueberries on the tree.
Purple is a vein that keeps us alive.

Katie Headdon (8)
Parkgate Primary School, Parkgate

The Ferret

As fast as lightning it charges
To break the neck of its prey.
Eyes as red as blood.
Its coat as white as snow.
Its strong bite can break a bond.

Gus Mackie (9)
Parkgate Primary School, Parkgate

Our House

'Go and get in the shower.'
'Why?'
'Because.'
'Why?'
'Because I say so.'
'Why?'
'Because I'm older.'
'Why?'
'Because it's shower time.'
'Why?'
'Just get in the shower.'
'Why?'
'I don't care now.'
'You're not going to get me to say why.'
'You just said why.'
'Oops!'

Jordan Murdock (9)
Parkgate Primary School, Parkgate

A Lion

Proudly walking into the jungle
With his silky coat and bushy mane,
His sharp pointed claws like knives.
He sees his prey out in the distance,
Sneakily crawling through the bushes,
Getting closer to his prey,
Suddenly pouncing at his feast
And dragging it back to his den.

Shola Neeson (9)
Parkgate Primary School, Parkgate

Love

Love is pink.
It tastes like melting chocolates.
Love smells like fresh roses.
It looks like hearts and flowers.
Love sounds like romantic music.
It feels like a soft cloud.

Alice Bell (11)
Parkgate Primary School, Parkgate

Fun

Fun is the colour of green like grass that sways repeatedly.
Fun sounds like laughter of children around the playground.
Fun tastes like sweets so sugary and sweet.
Fun smells like fresh air surrounding you in spring.
Fun looks like my sister jumping up and down on the trampoline.
Fun feels like your friends holding you up when you fall to the
                                                    ground laughing.
Fun reminds me of home where I'm always family-happy.

Hayleigh Quigg (11)
St Patrick's Primary School, Rasharkin

Fun

Fun . . . a bright yellow sun beaming down on the lake.
People laughing wildly at a straight-faced comedian.
Fluffiest, stickiest candyfloss at the theme park,
precarious on its stick.
Freshly baked Christmas cake, all spices and full of fruit.
An epic water fight at dusk last summertime.
Fun feels like my heart beating after playing tag,
on the first day I got a friend.

Mairead Carey (11)
St Patrick's Primary School, Rasharkin

Love Is . . .

A daffodil dancing in the wind - bopping, then waltzing in time.
A kind voice at tricky homework time - encouraging and
                                        helping along.
A creamy vanilla ice cream - smooth and ready to lick.
A waft of my favourite perfume - reviving and happy.
A mother correcting her cheeky child - firm but friendly too.
A clown throwing a pie at his partner - humorous and funny.
A rosy cheeked family running in the snow - joyful and fun-filled.

Shauna McKay (10)
St Patrick's Primary School, Rasharkin

Love

Love is always pink like the pinkest rose you've seen.
Love sounds like the church bells ringing as the newlyweds emerge.
Love tastes like sweet, juicy strawberries with a little topping
                                        of cream.
Love smells like beautiful scents and the most fragrant of flowers.
Love looks like a healthy heart pumping life in my veins.
Love feels like excitement, happiness and joy.

Sorcha Crawford (11)
St Patrick's Primary School, Rasharkin

Darkness

Darkness is the colour of black before the heavy rain.
Darkness sounds like pure peace with nothing moving around.
Darkness tastes like the smoke coming out of a lit chimney.
Darkness looks like a long hooded cloak gliding along.
Darkness feels like something is watching you and whispering.
Darkness reminds me of peace and quiet in a world of secrets
                                        and surprises.

Pierce McKeown (11)
St Patrick's Primary School, Rasharkin

Love

Love is the colour of pink like a radiant flower blowing in the breeze.
Love sounds like people telling you they love you
and won't let you go.
Love tastes sweet and nice like sugar sweetened tea.
Love smells like a gorgeous perfume being sprayed.
Love looks like two people sharing the gift of love.
Love feels like when you have butterflies in your stomach
when you meet someone you love.
Love reminds me of when my aunt got married
and the couple had their first dance with each other.

Catherine McGinty (11)
St Patrick's Primary School, Rasharkin

Darkness

Darkness is as black as the murky depths of the ocean.
Darkness sounds like Satan himself staring at you with an
evil chuckle.
Darkness smells like rotten flesh being eaten by predators.
Darkness tastes like sand mixed with scorpions and spiders.
Darkness looks like the face of the Grim Reaper coming to get you.
Darkness feels like standing in a graveyard at the stroke of midnight.
Darkness reminds me of war, death and all evil.

Fergus Quigg (11)
St Patrick's Primary School, Rasharkin

Darkness

The colour is black like the dark moon,
It sounds like the black of fear,
It tastes like dust,
It smells like a dark forest,
It looks like a dark cloud in the sky,
It feels like a soft, dark pillow,
It reminds me of the dark night at Hallowe'en.

Ryan Darragh (11)
St Patrick's Primary School, Rasharkin

Laughter

Laughter is red like a clown's cheeks after he gets a pie thrown at
his face.
Laughter sounds like a Mexican wave flying around the football pitch.
Laughter feels like someone tickling you with the biggest feather in
the world.
Laughter tastes like wibble wobble jelly melting in the sun.
Laughter looks like creased eyes on a smiling face.
Laughter reminds you of sunshine, lollipops and rainbows.

Adrian Walls (11)
St Patrick's Primary School, Rasharkin

Fun

Fun is bright blues and yellows like a victorious Rasharkin team.
It sounds like laughter, like a park full of fully-charged children.
Fun tastes like sweet, sugary candy and the thickest chocolate bars.
It smells like bubbles in a bath and a spray paint gun.
Fun looks like ridiculous rides at a funfair
And crashing waves on the shore.
It is irresistible and tempting.
Fun is simply fun!

Rhiannon O'Boyle (11)
St Patrick's Primary School, Rasharkin

Hunger Love

Love is red like a rose on a hot summer's day.
Love is the sound of happiness and joy.
Love is the taste of cinnamon.
Love is the smell of lovely perfume that my mum wears.
Love looks like joy on a child's face when he finds out good news.
Love feels like excitement when it's getting closer to my birthday.

Edel Kelly (10)
St Patrick's Primary School, Rasharkin

Silence

Silence is like the golden sun setting on the horizon of an
emerald-green meadow full of nodding daffodils.
There is never any silence, not even in a library.
There's the hum of the computer, the wafer thin pages turning.
For true silence you'd have to be in a vacuum.
Silence feels windless, a day like the day foxes like to hunt mice, when
the grass does not move.
Silence tastes like candyfloss, all soft and fluffy with no taste.
Silence looks like a glassy sea, not a ripple in sight
but soon to be broken.
Silence reminds me of weightless fluffy clouds drifting across the sky.
Silence smells like pot pourri roses, violets and tulips.

Seán Fleming (11)
St Patrick's Primary School, Rasharkin

Fear

Fear is black like claustrophobia when the doors of the world are
closing in on you and there is no room to breathe.
It sounds like violin strings being stretched and screeching
and the sound is being made by somebody who has never played
the instrument before.
It is as creepy as a hairy spider crawling up your spine.
The taste of fear is like burnt toast nearly on fire
and the crisp taste of it is all gone.
The look of it is a black burnt cauldron
and you're about to be dropped into it by a wicked witch.
Fear reminds me of a black cat ready to pounce on
a squeaky white mouse.
The smell of fear stinks like potatoes that are rotting.

Bronagh McGilligan (11)
St Patrick's Primary School, Rasharkin

Fear

Fear is the colour of black like a dark black cloud about to burst
and let the hard, cold rain fall down.
Fear sounds like a great, big booming sound coming from the distance
when you are left all alone.
It feels like a dark spirit lingering over your body trying to control you.
Fear tastes like bitterness when you just want to huddle up under the
covers of your bed and have a little cry.
Fear looks like blood running down your shin as you scream
with the pain!
Fear smells like old, rotten garlic dangling,
waiting to scare away vampires.
Fear reminds me of coldness, loneliness
and . . . *ghosts!*

Bronagh Hardy (11)
St Patrick's Primary School, Rasharkin

Silence

Silence is white like a silent cloud drifting across a silent sky.
Silence sounds like an empty room being abandoned by the world.
It feels like no one wants you and you've got to get out.
Silence tastes like a sick, empty taste, when you know you really badly
want to scream but just . . . can't.
It looks like an empty graveyard at midnight when you know spirits are
lurking about.
Silence reminds me of a room with no doors or windows
and no one notices.
It smells like a sweet yet slight smell of cinnamon scenting
an empty room.
Silence is . . .

Clodagh O'Kane (11)
St Patrick's Primary School, Rasharkin

Hunger

Hunger is black
Like the rats that carried the fleas,
That carried the plague.

Hunger sounds like
The moans and groans of people
As they starve.

Hunger tastes like
The last meal you get before you die,
You know it is of no use, but you eat it anyway.

Hunger smells like
The rotting of dead trees,
They're there, just there.

Hunger looks like
A pool of crystal clear water,
There's water, but no food.

Hunger feels like
Everything you ever wanted,
Is food on that list?

Patrick Mooney (11)
St Patrick's Primary School, Rasharkin

Silence

Silence is blue like a calm sea on a windless day,
It sounds like an empty room with no air in it,
It feels like emptiness, that awful feeling when you're all by yourself,
It tastes like a bun, sweet and relaxing,
It looks like a soundless world, as if no one lives there,
It reminds you of a puffy, white cloud silently moving by,
It smells like a new morning awakened and refreshed,
Silent but cool.

Shannon McLernon (11)
St Patrick's Primary School, Rasharkin

Laughter

Laughter is pink like your cheeks when you are laughing.
Laughter sounds like a crowd of people in a circus laughing
at a clown.
Laughter feels like your shoulders are shaking when someone
tells you a funny joke.
Laughter tastes like a lemon juice drink when you are
on the hot beach.
Laughter reminds me of the sun gleaming in space in silence.
Laughter smells like spring flowers swaying in the sun
on a hot summer's day.

Kristian Rogan (11)
St Patrick's Primary School, Rasharkin

Darkness

Darkness is black like dark, dark coal
being shoveled into a blazing fire.
It sounds like a werewolf howling beneath a full moon,
making an echo through the entire village.
Darkness feels like a grey, menacing cloud
spouting thunder and lightning strikes.
It tastes like cold mushrooms.
It looks like the deathly smoke from a cigarette.
Darkness is the smell of oil polluting the whole atmosphere.
It reminds me of a person alone
and terrified in a mysterious spooky cell.

Niamh McLernon (11)
St Patrick's Primary School, Rasharkin

Fear

Fear is the colour of black clouds at midnight with no stars to come out
and brighten up the sky.
It sounds like a raging tornado in the middle of complete darkness.
Fear feels like coming face to face with a grizzly bear,
jaws slobbering, ready to eat you.
It tastes like salty blood when you've bitten your gum.
Fear looks like a face twisted by terror.
It reminds you of a plane twisting, turning. Will it make it
to the runway?
Fear smells of a hot burning fire swallowing, gobbling everything
in its path.

Jack Quinn (11)
St Patrick's Primary School, Rasharkin

Laughter!

Laugher is like . . .
Orange jelly wobbling on the plate,
Adults roaring with laughter at a wedding speech,
Someone tickling you with a feather while you sleep,
It smells like you and your friends walking through a rose
garden singing happily,
Mmm, the sweet taste of candyfloss melting in your mouth,
It's like bubbles popping and out comes the sound of laughter,
It looks like a big, fat, merry, red-nosed clown in the circus!
That's what laughter is to me.

Shauna McIlfatrick (11)
St Patrick's Primary School, Rasharkin

Young Writers Information

We hope you have enjoyed reading this book - and that you will continue to enjoy it in the coming years.

If you like reading and writing poetry drop us a line, or give us a call, and we'll send you a free information pack.

Alternatively if you would like to order further copies of this book or any of our other titles, then please give us a call or log onto our website at www.youngwriters.co.uk

Young Writers Information
Remus House
Coltsfoot Drive
Peterborough
PE2 9JX

(01733) 890066